The Andrew R. Cecil Lectures on Moral Values in a Free Society

established by

The University of Texas at Dallas

Volume X

Previous Volumes of the Andrew R. Cecil Lectures
on Moral Values in a Free Society

RELIGION AND POLITICS

Religion
and
Politics

DALE BUMPERS
HAROLD J. BERMAN
CHRISTOPHER F. MOONEY
ANTHONY CHAMPAGNE
GEORGE ERIK RUPP
ANDREW R. CECIL

With an Introduction by
ANDREW R. CECIL

Edited by
W. LAWSON TAITTE

The University of Texas at Dallas
1989

Library of Congress Catalog Card Number 89-50241
International Standard Book Number 0-292-77044-8

Distributed by the University of Texas Press,
Box 7819, Austin, Texas 78712

FOREWORD

This volume of proceedings marks the tenth anniversary of the Andrew R. Cecil Lectures on Moral Values in a Free Society. The University of Texas at Dallas established this program in 1979 in order to provide a forum on its campus for the discussion of important issues facing our society. Each year since then the series has brought to the University prominent statesmen and scholars who have shared their ideas on selected topics with the academic community as well as the general public. At the end of this first decade of the Lectures, we can look back and note that the series has become a valued tradition for this institution. The distinguished lecturers in many fields who have participated in the program have contributed substantially to our understanding of the system of moral values on which our country was founded.

The University named this program for Dr. Andrew R. Cecil, the Distinguished Scholar in Residence at The University of Texas at Dallas. During his tenure as President of The Southwestern Legal Foundation, Dr. Cecil's innovative leadership moved that institution into the forefront of continuing legal education in the United States. When he retired from the Foundation as its Chancellor Emeritus, Dr. Cecil was asked by The University of Texas at Dallas to serve as its Distinguished Scholar in Residence, and the Cecil Lectures were initiated. It is appropriate that they honor a man who has been concerned throughout his career with the moral foundations of our society and has stressed his belief in the dignity and worth of every individual.

The theme of this tenth annual series of the

Lectures—held on the campus of the University from November 14 through 17, 1988—was "Religion and Politics." On behalf of the University of Texas at Dallas, I wish to express our gratitude to Senator Dale Bumpers, Professor Harold J. Berman, Father Christopher F. Mooney, Professor Anthony Champagne, President George Erik Rupp of Rice University, and Dr. Cecil for their willingness to share their ideas and for the thoughtful lectures that are preserved in these proceedings.

U.T. Dallas also wishes to express its appreciation to those who have helped make this program an important part of the life of the University, especially the contributors to the series. Through their support these donors enable us to continue this important project and to publish the proceedings of the series, thus assuring a wide audience and a permanent record of the ideas they contain.

I am sure that everyone who reads *Religion and Politics*, the Andrew R. Cecil Lectures on Moral Values in a Free Society Volume X, will be stimulated by the ideas in the six lectures it contains.

ROBERT H. RUTFORD, President
The University of Texas at Dallas
March, 1989

CONTENTS

INTRODUCTION

by

Andrew R. Cecil

After touring America on a government mission, Alexis de Tocqueville, the French statesman and writer, commented on this country's extraordinary religious nature: "On my arrival in the United States, the religious aspect of the country was the first thing that struck my attention. . . . There is no country in the world where the Christian religion retains a greater influence over the souls of men than in America."

This influence of religion had been part of the fabric of American life from the earliest days. According to the Mayflower Compact of November 11, 1620, the voyage of the Pilgrims was "undertaken for the Glory of God, and the Advancement of the Christian Faith." The Mayflower Compact describes itself as a covenant made "in the Presence of God." The colonists were propelled by religious fervor and came to this country in search of a religious liberty they had been denied in England or elsewhere.

Even before the American nation existed, the twin traditions of Christianity and liberty were well established on American soil. Pennsylvania may serve as an example of a colony where, from the beginning, deep Christian principles were combined with a respect for human liberty. The Frame of Government of Pennsylvania, adopted April 25, 1682, is prefaced with a rationale for constitutional government drawn

11

from Scripture, both Old and New Testaments. It refers to the fall of Adam, quotes the epistles of the Apostle Paul, and looks forward to the second "coming of the blessed *Second Adam*, the *Lord* from heaven."

William Penn's Frame of Government guarantees religious freedom to anyone who professes a belief in God. It provides

> "that all persons living in this province, who confess and acknowledge the one Almighty and eternal God, to be the Creator, Upholder and Ruler of the world; and that hold themselves obliged in conscience to live peaceably and justly in civil society, shall, in no ways, be molested or prejudiced for their religious persuasion, or practice, in matters of faith and worship, nor shall they be compelled, at any time, to frequent or maintain any religious worship, place or ministry whatever."

These declarations of religious freedom prepared the way for the broader guarantee embodied a century later in the Constitution of the United States and the Bill of Rights. The first and most immediate purpose of the adoption of the First Amendment was the belief that a union of government and religion tends to destroy government and degrade religion. This belief was expressed by the court almost 100 years later: "United with government, religion never rises above the merest superstition; united with religion, government never rises above the merest despotism; and all history shows us that the more widely and completely they are separated the better it is for both." (*Board of Education of Cincinnati v. Minor*, 23 Ohio St. 211, 13 Am. Rep. 233 [1872].) This separation of the domains of government and religion was designed to give each realm its proper place in the lives of the citizens of our country.

Belief in religious freedom and in the separation of church and state does not preclude the conviction that religion's moral code bears on our laws and forms an operative part of our social obligations. Our courts have taken a position that Christianity entered and influenced, more or less, all our institutions, customs, and relations, as well as our individual modes of thinking and acting.

> "It is so involved in our social nature, that even those among us who reject Christianity, cannot possibly get clear of its influence, or reject those sentiments, customs and principles which it has spread among the people, so that, like the air we breathe, they have become the common stock of the whole country, and essential elements of its life." (*Mohney v. Cook*, 26 Pa. 342 [1855].)

The founders of this country and the courts have repeatedly stressed that in any action a magistrate takes in regard to the belief or disbelief of religious principles, there is always the danger of trampling on the rights of conscience and destroying religious liberty. Those who wrote our Constitution never sought to make proselytes by coercion, but they did not preclude the application of religious and moral principles to public life.

Our constitutional heritage draws a fine distinction between what properly belongs to the church and what to the state. This heritage instructs us that the church does not need an alliance with the state to encourage its growth nor laws to enforce it. Nor does the state need an alliance with the church to carry out its political goals.

Senator Dale Bumpers, in his lecture "The Constitution and Our Religious Values: A Politician's View," expresses his alarm at recent attempts to amend the Constitution and his fears that such attempts could upset the delicate balance between church and state that our forefathers established. He also deplores the manner in which issues of religion and patriotism were raised in the 1988 presidential election. For him, the essence of religious freedom is freedom of choice—the right to dissent even on behalf of an unpopular cause.

Senator Bumpers sees the proper role of religious values in political life as one of moral guidance. The great problems that our nation and our world face can be addressed only by those who draw their strength from religious values. Conscience leads us to assume our responsibility for the proper stewardship of our society. The real issues in discharging these responsibilities, the Senator argues, are often blurred or distracted from public consciousness by misguided political leaders who loudly stress unimportant problems or offer the wrong solutions to those problems that truly are important.

The connection between religious conviction and moral purpose of which Senator Bumpers speaks has long been a part of the American tradition. In the early years of the nineteenth century, numerous decisions of state courts declared Christianity to be a part of common law we inherited from England. Sir William Blackstone, the illustrious English jurist, argued in his famous *Commentaries on the Laws of England* that providence revealed its laws in the Holy Scriptures, which are to be considered part of the original law of nature, and "they tend in all their consequence to man's felicity."

In his lecture "The Religion Clauses of the First Amendment in Historical Perspective," Professor Harold J. Berman delves even farther into the historical relationship between Christianity and the state, examining that relationship from the earliest days of Christian history through the time of the founding of our republic. From the period of Constantine's elevation of Christianity to the official religion of the Roman empire to the present, the general trend has been for leaders of both church and state to recognize that a separation of the two powers is in fact beneficial to both. But in this progression, the founding of the United States marked a new era by declaring as public policy for the first time the principle of neutrality of the state toward religious matters.

Professor Berman recognizes the interpenetration between religious values and public issues and gives many examples to demonstrate that in the early days of the United States there was a consensus of many authorities that Christian values permeated all our institutions. He also shows, however, that within the last two generations a more clear-cut division between church and state has evolved. He does not think it possible or even desirable that this evolution should be reversed, yet he does believe that it is possible that government and religion can find new ways

of cooperation that do not violate the spirit of the
Constitution.

We should be reminded that since there is no
established church or religion in the United States,
even when Christianity is held to be within the
common law, our Constitution offers freedom of
religious worship to all and does not prevent or
restrain the formation of any opinions or the profession of any religious sentiments. In the history of our
nation, there have been many movements toward the
accommodation of such religious sentiments to public
life, as long as there is no real danger of establishment
of a state church.

In the spirit of such accommodation, President
Washington proclaimed November 26, 1789, a day of
thanksgiving to offer "our prayers and supplications to
the Great Lord and Ruler of Nations, and beseech
Him to pardon our national and other transgressions."
References to our religious heritage are found in the
statutorily prescribed national motto, "In God We
Trust," and in the Pledge of Allegiance to the
American flag, where we are "One Nation under
God." There are countless other illustrations of the
accommodation of religion to American public life
that support the opinion expressed by Justice Douglas
that "we are a religious people whose institutions
presuppose a Supreme Being."

In his lecture "The Accommodation of Religious
Conscience," Father Christopher F. Mooney, S. J.,
examines the question of how it is possible to reconcile the ideal of benevolence toward the free exercise
of religion (which is the provision of one clause of the
First Amendment) with that of the separation of

church and state (which is the provision of the other clause). In tracing the history of the founding of our republic, Fr. Mooney finds ample evidence of the willingness of even those Founding Fathers most adamant in their desire for a strict separation of church and state to find ways to accommodate religious belief and practice with public life. The evidence of just how much interaction they envisioned as allowable is ambiguous, but it is clear that they relied on the multiplicity of religious traditions in America to serve as a protection against the domination of any one religion.

Fr. Mooney traces the history of the recent courtroom struggles on such issues as classroom prayer and the teaching of evolution in public schools. Like Professor Berman, he argues that the increasing diversity of attitudes toward religion and of religious practice and belief make it impossible to return to the standards of accommodation that prevailed in the past. He does believe, however, that it is possible to teach *about* religion in public schools without violating constitutional principles and that there may be other areas of accommodation that may be found without violating the basic principle of the separation of church and state.

In discussing these areas of accommodation, we may note signs of a shift in the Supreme Court's position toward official acknowledgement of the role of religion in American life and the expansion of such accommodation. In *Lynch v. Donnelly* in March 1984, for instance, the Supreme Court held that the Constitution does not require complete separation of church and state; it affirmatively mandates accommo-

dation, not merely tolerance, and forbids hostility
toward any. "There is an unbroken history," wrote the
Court, "of official acknowledgement by all three
branches of government of the role of religion in
American life from at least 1789." The concept of a
"wall" of separation between church and state is,
therefore, "a useful metaphor" but "is not a wholly
accurate description of the practical aspects of the
relationship that in fact exists." (104 S. Ct. 1355, 1359
[1984].)

Professor Anthony Champagne, in his lecture
"Religion as a Political Interest Group," maintains
that the ideal of the separation of church and state
must be seen against the reality of the strong influence that religious belief and practice have in our
society. He shows that the United States is far and
away the most religious society among all the
developed nations. Religious belief plays an important role in the decisions—including political
decisions—of most Americans. Because such deeply
held beliefs shape the consciences of individuals, they
also inevitably shape decisions that are made on the
basis of conscience by public figures such as legislators and judges.

Of course, we must differentiate between religion,
which as a system of interior belief cannot be wholly
separated from any action or decision of an individual,
and the organized church. It is the entanglements of
the organized church in public life that the First
Amendment was designed to protect. Professor
Champagne also examines the degree to which some
churches have become involved in the political
process as lobbying groups. Here, too, there is a long

history of political activism on the part of clergy on behalf of many causes during the course of the life of our nation—we need mention only the abolition of slavery, the prohibition of alcohol, and the establishment of civil rights for all Americans as a few such issues in which individual churches and whole denominations were actively involved. In our own day, the issue of abortion is the one in which the organized church is most visibly active.

We can see that the injection of moral principle into public life and even the involvement of the organized church in political life are not new trends in the history of our country. What is new, as several of our lecturers point out, is the heightened awareness of the deep differences in the beliefs that the various citizens of our nation hold. These differences raise the question whether it is still possible to claim that our society is built on shared moral values, when there is such diversity and even division within it.

Rice University President George Rupp, in his lecture "From Civil Religion to Public Faith," proposes a way in which it is still possible for individuals with deeply held but not completely reconcilable beliefs to try to find some common moral ground. President Rupp recognizes that the days are gone forever when the United States could assume that there was a commonly held belief system, which he calls "civil religion." He refers to a generalized Protestantism acceptable to most citizens and, as mentioned above, constituting a part of the common law. He does not lament those vanished days, since such civil religion is at best watered down and at worst oppressive to some.

Far from being discouraged at the attenuation of such civil religion, President Rupp sees the present pluralism of our culture as a magnificent opportunity. Americans still have the right, indeed the responsibility, to bring their deepest moral and religious insights to bear on public issues. Now, however, such insights must be tested by the strictest standards of self-criticism and comparative scrutiny. In attempting to develop what President Rupp terms a "public faith," it will be impossible for anyone to claim personal access to absolute truth.

We should point out that there is a growing pressure coming from the political force known as the Religious New Right to augment the existing accommodations between religion and public life that our constitutional tradition has established. The goal of this movement is to turn America into a "Christian Republic," with religious beliefs incorporated into all political decisions and activities. No one denies the right of religious people to become involved in political activities, but religion should not be confused with the attempts of organized religion to give directions in politics from the pulpit or with claims by politicians that they have a special relationship with God. When religion is used as a political weapon, the fundamental principles of the church become obscured by the belief that some political or economic view is ordained by God, and, therefore, adherence to that point of view is construed as a test of loyalty to the church. This is a corruption of the proper role of religion in our public life. No one should claim to be God's spokesman.

In my lecture on "Loyalty," I tried to answer more

clearly the question: "What is the proper relationship between our loyalties to the state and our loyalties to the church?" The United States was unique, at the time of its founding, in that its cohesiveness was based on the "self evident truth: that all men are endowed by certain unalienable rights and that governments derive their just powers from the consent of the governed." The writers of the Declaration of Independence found an "American purpose" to which they pledged their common loyalty "with a firm reliance on the protection of divine Providence."

It cannot be denied that in this country religious values pervade the fabric of our national life. But it is also true that it is up to each individual to make up his own mind on public, political issues. Competing loyalties to the state and to the church should not debilitate the spirit of the "American purpose." When competing loyalties to the church and to the state create tensions, we should be reminded that the prime objective of the ministry of the church is to help us to turn Christian principles into attitudes that motivate our conduct. These attitudes may be summarized by Martin Luther's two formulas—first, that a Christian is a perfectly free lord of all, subject to no one else, and, second, that a Christian is a perfectly free servant of all, subject to everyone, accountable to God.

In conclusion, we may say that in the 1988 Lectures on Moral Values in a Free Society the theme is repeatedly emphasized that man was meant to be free and to have the ability to stand unimpeded by the state or the organized church in the light of his Creator as he sees fit to discern that light. The "wall of

separation" created by the First Amendment to the
Constitution of the United States was intended to
keep government, politicians claiming to be religious
leaders, and religious leaders involved in politics from
intruding into that light—and not to keep that light
from illuminating the fields of public discourse, as too
many have tried to interpret that intent.

THE CONSTITUTION AND
OUR RELIGIOUS VALUES:
A POLITICIAN'S VIEW

by

Dale Bumpers

Dale Bumpers

First elected to the U.S. Senate in 1974, Senator Dale Bumpers is now in his third term as a Democratic Senator from Arkansas. He was reelected in 1986 with 62 percent of the vote. Before joining the U.S. Senate, Bumpers served two terms as Governor of Arkansas, where he reorganized the state government and became one of the most popular governors in the state's history.

After serving in the U.S. Marine Corps for three years during World War II, Senator Bumpers did his undergraduate work at the University of Arkansas and later received his law degrees from Northwestern University. Prior to entering politics, Bumpers lived in his home town of Charleston, where he practiced law; operated a small hardware, furniture, and appliance business; raised Angus cattle; and had several other business interests. During those years Bumpers was also active in community affairs, serving as city attorney, president of the school board, and president of the chamber of commerce.

In the Senate, Bumpers is a leader on arms control issues, has consistently voted for stringent measures to get our budget deficits under control, and is a staunch defender of the U.S. Constitution. He is a strong advocate of rural America, small business, and farmers, and a tireless supporter of measures to protect the environment.

The Senator serves as the Chairman of the Senate Small Business Committee, is a ranking member of the Energy and Natural Resources Committee and Chairman of its Subcommittee on Parks and Public Lands, and serves on the Appropriations Committee where he chairs the Subcommittee on the Legislative Branch.

THE CONSTITUTION AND OUR
RELIGIOUS VALUES: A POLITICIAN'S VIEW

by

Dale Bumpers

It is my pleasure to participate in this great lecture series that honors the name of my good friend Andrew R. Cecil. I am very familiar with this lecture series and with *Democracy: Its Strengths and Weaknesses*, the volume containing last year's fine lectures. I was particularly struck by some of Dr. Cecil's introductory comments, which I think are worth repeating here:

> "Throughout recent history, we have witnessed the ascent and eventual fall of many dogmas that tried to offer a vision of a perfect society. In order not to suffer the fate of these passing dogmas, each generation, through its judges and duly elected representatives, has to breathe new life into democracy—this forceful principle of political action capable of adjusting itself to the changes that constantly occur in any society. The strength of democracy lies in the ability to rise to challenges. . . ." (W. Lawson Taitte, ed., *Democracy: Its Strengths and Weaknesses*, The University of Texas at Dallas, 1988, p. 25.)

As I prepared my remarks, I thought about these profound words of wisdom and the strength of our constitutional system. It is my firm belief that the brilliance of our system stems from our great Constitution, which has allowed us to be the longest living democracy in history. And as a member of the U. S. Senate, I fervently hope that I am part of breathing new life into our democracy each day rather than tearing it down as some would do.

The Brilliance of Our Constitution

Many of you may have read one or more of the books of Barbara Tuchman, the eminent historian. The one I really like best—and it probably ought to be required reading for everyone in the United States before they finish their formal schooling—is called *The March of Folly: From Troy to Vietnam.* (Knopf, 1984.) The thesis of this book is that for 4000 years mankind has been trying to govern itself and for 4000 years we have kept shooting ourselves in the foot. The author reviews a litany of eras of history and describes how the wrong decisions were made, despite the fact that there was at the time a sane and rational voice saying, "This is nonsense, don't do it." She judges everything not by hindsight but by whether there was a sane alternative at the time; she asks whether someone was advocating a sensible solution during the period in question.

For example, we all remember the great Trojan War when the Greeks built the Trojan horse. Legend has it that they sailed their ships behind an island to make the Trojans think they had gone, but instead the Greeks left the horse with their best warriors inside it. The next morning when the Trojans opened the gate, there was the horse, and they did not know what to do. They said, "Well, this is obviously a tribute to one of the gods; we've got to let the horse in or we'll make the gods angry." One Trojan, Laocoön, warned, "What have the Greeks ever done for Troy? This is a trick. If we let that horse in here, we're going to be sorry." The others shouted him down in nothing flat. As a matter of fact, two serpents came up out of the sea and choked him to death. That was all the proof the others needed. Enter the horse. End of Troy.

Tuchman gives a whole host of other examples. George III had thoughtful people around him advising, "Get your feet off the colonies' neck and we can keep them as our own." He was not having any of that, and the rest is history. Napoleon was advised, "Don't try to invade Russia." Hitler was also advised, "Don't try to invade Russia." They were having none of that. In World War II, Yamamoto sat at the council of the war table and said, "I can destroy the American fleet at Pearl Harbor, but if you think we can defeat the United States, you're daydreaming. The best we could do would be to bomb Pearl Harbor, and take out as much of their fleet as possible." He was shouted down in that council, and the rest is history. And Dwight Eisenhower, maybe not the greatest President but a fairly good general, said, "Don't ever get bogged down in a war in Asia." So we promptly got bogged down in Asia in the most debilitating experience in the history of this country.

But Tuchman concludes that the United States is still the last best hope for man's ability to govern himself because of our great Constitution, which has made us the oldest living democracy, with the second-oldest living organic law, next to that of Iceland, of any nation on earth. Alfred North Whitehead, the great English philosopher, said that the two things that man had done about as well as could possibly be done were the reign of Caesar Augustus and the drafting of the United States Constitution. And Arthur Schlesinger, the preeminent historian, said that the assemblage of minds in Philadelphia 200 years ago was probably the greatest in the history of the world.

As I stand in the United States Senate, I agree with Barbara Tuchman, and I agree with Alfred North Whitehead, and I agree with Arthur Schlesinger. I believe that anybody who proposes to change this great document has the burden of proving that change is absolutely necessary to secure our freedoms.

It is interesting to me that we seldom hear the lunatic fringe of politics in this country say anything in defense of the Constitution. They do not like it; it is just that simple. There has been a veritable assault on the Constitution in the past few years. It is almost unbelievable, but in the past twelve years more than 1800 resolutions have been introduced to amend the Constitution. Most of them were introduced merely so some Senator or Congressman could send a press release back home saying, "I'm against abortion," or "I'm for prayer in school," or "I'm for a balanced budget." Happily for all of us, none of these resolutions has passed both houses by the requisite two-thirds majority. Mercifully, the only serious debates on these proposed constitutional amendments during my fourteen years in the Senate were those in 1983 on the one to require a balanced federal budget and in 1984 on the one to establish prayer in school.

The long and tedious procedures for amending our Constitution are not accidental. Madison, Hamilton, Adams, all our founders, agreed that people have to have time to think these things over. Amending the Constitution is intended to be a "leaden-footed process." As such, it has forced the zealots in the right wing to adopt a different strategy. They try by legislation, which requires a simple majority vote, to strip our federal courts of jurisdiction to hear controversial issues. They do this because it is a painfully long, laborious, and tedious process to amend the Constitution. They also know that if the American people are given, as the amendment process contemplates, several years to analyze a particular proposal— especially something the zealots would come up with—it is not likely to be ratified.

These court-stripping proposals say that no federal court shall have jurisdiction, for example, over any case where the issue is whether prayer in school is voluntary, over any case involving busing of school children, or over scores of other issues I could name.

Incidentally, to digress for a moment, I have the distinction of being the only southern Senator to vote against the Constitutional amendment on prayer in school, and if you had heard my opponent when I ran for re-election in 1986 you would have thought I was the only Senator, period, to do so. He brought it up every speech he gave. And I was the only southern Senator to vote against Jesse Helms's court-stripping provision, which would have taken jurisdiction away from all federal courts to require busing over a certain distance, even if the community wanted it. That vote was probably the most deadly politically I have ever made.

But let me get back to my main point, which is that these court-stripping proposals are really backdoor constitutional amendments in disguise, and they require only a majority vote and presidential signature. Are they constitutional? If you study Article III of the Constitution, it is not absolutely clear. Article III says, and I am paraphrasing here, that a Supreme Court is created, as are such other courts as Congress from time to time wishes to establish. It also gives Congress the power to determine the jurisdiction of the lower federal courts and the appellate jurisdiction of the Supreme Court.

If you read *Ex parte McCardle*, the 1869 case in which the Supreme Court upheld a legislative attempt by Congress to remove the Court's jurisdiction over a pending case, you will discover that it is not entirely clear that the Supreme Court will rule a court-stripping provision unconstitutional. It is my own studied opinion that if the Supreme Court ever does declare that Congress has the right to take away court jurisdiction over basic constitutional guarantees, you can make a dart board out of the Constitution. It will be a eunuch.

No one likes court-ordered busing, for example, but what if it is the only remedy that will work to eliminate the unconstitutional discrimination? To deny the courts' jurisdiction is to allow unconstitu-

tional discrimination to exist. And if we cut off jurisdiction over busing, what is to keep us from stripping
jurisdiction to hear school prayer cases or abortion
cases or even search-and-seizure cases?

These efforts are not new. Court-stripping bills
flourished in the late 1860s after the Civil War and in
the 1930s as this nation was fighting its way out of the
Great Depression. Again in the 1950s, several such
bills were introduced, and I mentioned that they have
again flourished in the late 1970s and the 1980s.

But I cannot say it loud enough or often enough:
These efforts to amend the Constitution by simple
majority were wrong in the 1860s, wrong in the
1930s, wrong in the 1950s, and wrong today! It
requires men and women of courage to say so and say
it loudly, regardless of the personal political con-
sequences.

The Corruption of Power

James Madison went to the Constitutional Convention and, if nothing else, proved what I always tell
high school students, that knowledge is power. He
went with a hip pocket of papers that he had very
carefully considered, and he was bound and determined to write a new document, although the only
mandate was to amend the Articles of Confederation.
Madison knew that you could not have 13 different
states raising their own militias, coining their own
money, going their separate ways. As a matter of fact,
many of the 13 colonies had established religions at
that time. He therefore understood that we needed a

new fundamental document; he also understood the frailties of men, and especially of politicians.

Alexander Hamilton, as you know, wanted a very strong central government and would have given the President literally royal powers. When the Constitution was finally written, however, Madison had more say than anyone else, happily for all of us. What the Founders tried to do in Philadelphia was to grant as much freedom as possible to the individual but to limit the power of the majority or of individuals to take away the basic guarantees granted to all, including the minority. While we would all be free, the government would make sure that one person did not have the right to take those same liberties away from somebody else. Madison knew that power corrupts, that absolute power corrupts absolutely, and that if you give a man the power, the first thing he wants is for you to dance to his tune, march to his drummer, believe as he believes. Throughout history, every time man has been given absolute power, he has demanded absolute conformity. When you read Barbara Tuchman's book, you will see instance after instance of that happening.

I can remember a two-hour private conversation in 1976 with the Shah of Iran in his palace. I wish everyone could have seen it. The trappings of that office were unbelievable. Just before I was in Tehran, I had read in the *New York Times* that the Shah had possibly 300,000 political prisoners; since I did not have anything to lose, I confronted him with it. He said, "Oh, the *New York Times* is such a terrible newspaper. They keep printing things like that." I asked, "Well, your majesty, how many do you have?" He said, "Oh, perhaps 3,300." He seemed to know precisely. But he said, "You know they're communist. And we have a law that says you may not be communist." Well, of course he was the law. He was the absolute power, and he was, I believe, absolutely corrupt.

Religion and Patriotism

The Pledge of Allegiance issue of George Bush's 1988 presidential campaign was and is very troubling to me. I am reading a book now—a little bit of tough sledding but interesting—called the *Trial of Socrates* by I. F. Stone. I recommend it to you. In a nutshell, it tells the story of Socrates, seventy years old and in his declining years; at that time, he was considered eccentric because he searched for truth, and a lot of the truths that were self-evident were not very popular. The Athenians had the first democracy, as you know and for twenty-five years that democracy had been going downhill because they had increasingly become less tolerant of free thought and free speech. Finally, the Athenians brought in Socrates, this great and brilliant scholar, and tried him for treason. The dialogue at trial was essentially like this:

"What do you believe?"

"I believe in the truth."

"Is that what you spend all your waking hours believing?"

"Of course?"

"Do you love the truth?"

"Yes."

"Well, do you love Athens?"

"Of course."

And then the key question, "Which do you love more?"

And Socrates said, "There's no contradiction. I love both. If I find the truth, Athens benefits."

They were not having any of that. Now, you see, Socrates, like Jesus, could have saved himself. All he had to do was mutter the right words. But Socrates was a pretty acerbic, caustic guy anyway, and was not about to let the Athenians bend his mind, so they sentenced him to death and let him commit suicide.

I think of the story of Socrates when I consider this Pledge of Allegiance issue George Bush raised during the campaign. I am sure you remember that he pilloried Michael Dukakis for vetoing legislation that would have required the reciting of the Pledge of Allegiance each morning in Massachusetts public schools and would have made criminals out of teachers who refused to lead the Pledge. Bush said, "Somehow or other I would have found a way to sign that bill." Well now, how do you do that? If you are sworn to uphold and defend the Constitution, how do you find a way to sign a bill that in the opinion of most legal scholars in this country is palpably unconstitutional? To do so, you would have to think that politics is more important than the Constitution. One time I asked Senator Strom Thurmond of South Carolina during Senate debate, "What does it mean to you when you put your left hand on the Bible and your right hand in the air and say, 'I will protect and defend the Constitution of the United States?' Does that mean only when you agree, or even when it's unpopular?"

Symbolism is important. Michael Dukakis realized that too late. The Pledge of Allegiance is important to the people of this country. But it was a shameful, shameful thing to trivialize the Pledge of Allegiance which all of us love, just as we love the national anthem—even though I wish it were in a little lower key so I could sing it. I talk about the Pledge of Allegiance with college and high school students every chance I get, because the issue as it came up in the campaign is widely misunderstood. Many think that Dukakis was trying to outlaw the Pledge of Allegiance. The truth of the matter is, he was trying to follow the dictates of a 6-2 opinion of the Massachusetts Supreme Court that held, under the *West Virginia State Board of Education v. Barnette* (319 U.S. 624 [1943]) decision, that, clearly, teachers cannot be required to lead the Pledge of Allegiance.

As a former trial lawyer, and keeping in mind the Socrates trial, I can only think what a courtroom setting would be with George Bush as the prosecutor and Michael Dukakis as witness:

"Do you love the national anthem?"
"Yes."
"Do you sing it?"
"Yes."
"Do you love the Pledge of Allegiance?"
"Yes."
"Do you get goosebumps when you say it?"
"You bet."

"Well, how many?"

These people seem to think that by a rote saying of the Pledge of Allegiance you force patriotism. It never works and never will. Justice Jackson in that *Barnette* decision, which involved two sisters who were members of Jehovah's Witnesses and who refused to participate in the saying of the Pledge of Allegiance because they thought it was sacrilegious, wrote as follows: "To believe that patriotism will not flourish if patriotic ceremonies are voluntary and spontaneous instead of compulsory routine, is to make an unflattering estimate of the appeal of our institutions to free minds." (*Ibid.*, 641).

Religious Freedom

New York Governor Mario Cuomo, in a great speech at Notre Dame last year on the separation of church and state, said, "I preserve my right to be a Catholic by preserving your right to believe as a Jew, a Protestant, a non-believer, or as anything else you choose. We know that the price of seeking to force our beliefs on others is that they might someday force theirs on us."

The Falwells, the Swaggarts, the Bakkers, and the Robertsons are frenzied because they cannot make us believe as they believe. We all know that the separation of church and state, the Establishment and the Free Exercise Clauses of the First Amendment mean that you are not only free to practice religion, you are free from religion if that is your choice. I am a devout Methodist but you need not be. We are a pluralistic nation where men and women can worship as they please, according to the dictates of their own consciences and not the conscience of Jesse Helms or Pat Robertson.

Religious Values in Politics

Clearly, it was never the intent of the Founders to deny religion a role in shaping public policy in America. Even Jefferson's wall of separation, enshrined in the First Amendment, was never intended to be such a barrier. In fact, the very tension between the Establishment and Free Exercise Clauses in the First Amendment has created an atmosphere in America of both unprecedented religious freedom and vigorous religious activism.

We are looking over an abyss—the insanity of the arms race continues; we poison ourselves with chemical and nuclear waste, and even our drinking water is impure; in an act of shocking immorality by any standard, we continue to burden our children and grandchildren with a mountain of debt they will never dig out of; and we are facing perhaps the most vicious disease in the history of mankind, AIDS. Our remarkable computer technology encourages foolish dreamers to wish for a nuclear shield, an umbrella to protect us from nuclear attack; we nearly double defense spending while slashing student loans and nutrition programs and granting huge tax cuts for the wealthiest 1 percent in our society. We have the technology to keep people alive almost forever, but how do we make the godlike decision of when to pull the plug? We are shamelessly last among all developed nations in the rate of infant mortality—it is nothing short of scandalous. How have we allowed ourselves into this quagmire?

We in Congress desperately need moral guidance. May we look to religion and our Judaeo-Christian heritage? We are foolish if we do not. Religion, as a major source of values, has been the glue that has held our society together.

The enormity of our problems demands that we bring to bear the kind of character, conscience, and fiber that draw their strength from our religious values. Charles Whittier, a scholar on religion and public policy at the Library of Congress, writes, "Families, churches, neighborhoods, and voluntary associations of every kind generate and sustain values which find inevitable expression in public affairs and in the life of the community as a whole. . . ." I would think that no one would seriously argue with the responsibility of a lawmaker to rely upon his own values and those of the community as a whole in carrying out his legislative responsibilities. "[T]he values that inform our public discourse are inseparably related to . . . religious traditions," write Peter Berger and Richard Neuhaus. (*To Empower People: The Role of Mediating Structures in Public Policy*, American Enterprise Institute, 1977, p. 30.)

According to polls taken by the Williamsburg Charter Foundation, people in this country understand the influence of religious values on political decisions. They want us elected officials to consider religious principles, but not dogma or doctrine, in reaching our decisions, and they want us to use common sense.

That prayer in school amendment I mentioned earlier was a very tough vote for me. Ninety-two percent of the people in my state, Arkansas, wanted me to vote for it. But the people of Arkansas are no different from the people of Texas or California or Arizona or Idaho or any other state in accepting common sense and rational, sane explanations of why a legislative proposal is good or bad. That is not to say that I am always right, but I have a duty when I cast my votes, especially those that are unpopular, to go home and talk sense to my people, and I have found that they are always receptive to common sense.

I got 63 percent of the vote in the 1986 election, although my opponent started the campaign with a $200,000 media blitz against "the only Senator to vote against letting our little children pray down at the school house." And who do you think the leaders against that amendment were in the Senate? Jack Danforth of Missouri, an ordained Episcopal priest, and Mark Hatfield of Oregon, who probably holds honorary doctorates from more religious schools than anybody else in the United States. They knew, and I knew, that the passage of that amendment would have guaranteed us less religious freedom, not more, because it would have allowed governments to adopt official mandatory prayers for our children to repeat.

You know, sometimes I wonder how much of this whole right wing political and religious agenda is driven by money. There is no money in preaching peace and equality. There is no money in saying I

believe in helping the poor, no money in being for all
the things Christ talked about in the Sermon on the
Mount.

I went to see a great musical at the Kennedy Center
the other night called *Les Miserables*, which some of
you have seen. It starts off with all these people in
debtors' prison crying out, "Look down, look down,
have mercy if you can. Look down, look down," and I
believe the next line is, "Give a helping hand." That
is one of the clearest religious values permeating our
Judaeo-Christian heritage. Yet the money for the
Swaggarts and the Falwells and all the rest is not
donated to help the down and out; it comes from
being against busing, abortion, and homosexuality,
and so those issues are their agenda.

The social and political lessons of the Old Testament seldom quoted by the mandatory school prayer
advocates were quoted by the psalmist who said,
"Defend the poor and fatherless. Do justice to the
afflicted and needy." Hubert Humphrey made what I
consider a great statement when he said, "The test of
government is how it treats its children in the dawn of
life, old people in the twilight of life, and the poor in
the shadows of life." In my personal life and in the
Senate, I combine my own religious principles, or the
great truths that have stood the test to time as I understand them, and my understanding of history. Incidentally, I would not vote for any man or woman
who did not know history. And I would not vote for
anyone who did not have a sense of humor, while I am
at it.

If I were going to summarize the Constitution, I
would say that it demonstrates that each one of us

counts. Is that not our Judaeo-Christian belief and guide? Is not a nuclear holocaust the ultimate betrayal of God's command to us and the ultimate betrayal of the principles of virtually every religion? And are not our infant mortality rate and our child poverty rate crimes against God?

The Constitution does not deal specifically with a whole host of issues. It guarantees personal liberty, but it does not deal with a variety of important policy issues, for example, with the mountain of debt, which, as I mentioned previously, I consider to be immoral, that we are forcing off on our children and grandchildren. Would not the values of all established religions condemn this kind of failure of responsibility? And is not our mindless destruction of the environment also a breach of God's intentions for us and a betrayal of our stewardship? And can a democracy survive while it allows the wealthiest 5 percent of the nation to continue to accumulate a bigger slice of the pie, virtually all of which is at the expense of the bottom 4 percent?

We all have some fear of communism. Any historian will attest that we must have a viable middle class to keep communism from ever taking root. One of the things we have always said about Mexico is that it has a big, broad middle class and that that will be enough to keep communism away. Now the middle class of Mexico is being eroded. And the middle class, particularly the lower middle class, is also being eroded in the United States. Franklin Roosevelt said one time that "the groans of the pocketbooks of the rich are louder than the groans of the bellies of the hungry." It is now those same pocketbooks, in the form of campaign financing, that dictate public policy in this country. One of the reasons courage often fails politicians is that they know where the money has to come from in the next campaign.

Diversions vs. Fundamental Issues

Amos lived almost 800 years before Christ and was the first of the Old Testament prophets who spoke about a God who is universal, that is, for all mankind. Amos was a blunt but powerful preacher, and he spoke of justice. He looked out at his people in Judea and saw how they were treating the poor, cheating them and exploiting them, and he lashed out: "Let justice roll down like waters and righteousness like an ever-flowing stream." He told his congregation that God does not want a lot of pious homage, and He does not want clanging cymbals, noisy gongs, and loud singing to cover up injustice and unfairness in any society.

Jesus, of course, also took up the banner of justice. In His very first sermon, He declared that He had been anointed by God to bring good news to the poor, to set the captives free, and to bring liberty to those who are oppressed. And it goes without saying that the ideals of justice of Martin Luther King, Jr., were inspired by his religious faith.

Amos, Jesus, and Martin Luther King, Jr., never allowed themselves to be distracted by clanging cymbals or noisy gongs, and we must not allow attention from the real issues to be diverted by the loud distractions of the far right. Do you remember the Trilateral Commission? One of the big issues in the

1980 campaign was this Trilateral Commission; nobody knew what it was, but everybody assumed it was hatched up in the Kremlin. It was actually an organization founded by the Rockefeller brothers to try to improve relations among Japan, the United States, and Canada. And when did you ever hear of the Trilateral Commission again after the votes were counted?

In 1960, when Richard Nixon and Jack Kennedy opposed each other, the distraction was Quemoy and Matsu, two small islands off the coast of China. You never heard of Quemoy and Matsu again after the votes were counted. And this year it has been the American Civil Liberties Union, which will continue to be around, although we have not heard George Bush talk much about it since the election.

We will not hear anything more about the Pledge of Allegiance, and we will soon forget about the Massachusetts furlough policies. Virtually every state in the country has such a policy, and Texas has a more liberal one than Massachusetts has. Fourteen thousand inmates were granted furlough from federal prisons on Ronald Reagan's watch, 5000 of them drug dealers. So the furlough policy, which arguably helped to defeat Michael Dukakis, is no longer an issue. It was simply a distraction, and now we are left with the real issues. How are we going to balance this budget, and how are we going to deal with Japan and the trade deficit? Are we going to continue our current practice until the Japanese own all the real estate and are both our employers and our landlords? Are we going to deal sensibly with Gorbachev, or are we going to allow the far right to dictate the foreign policy agenda so that the nuclear holocaust becomes almost inevitable?

Most people I know were unhappy with the choices available to them during this election. They do consider crime, a strong defense, and patriotism to be important viscerally, but they also know viscerally that they are being had. They understand what the real issues are. They yearn for Harry Truman, but on today's television Harry Truman would not make the first cut in a primary. He was not a media candidate. Lloyd Bentsen could not make the first cut in the primaries in 1976, and now almost everybody wishes they could have voted for him this year.

A president of one of the biggest corporations in America recently said to me, "Senator, I believe if somebody would have just laid it out like it is, told us what we have to do, I believe he'd have been the next President of the United States." I said, "Why don't you go talk to Bruce Babbitt about that? He didn't make the first cut either, although he told the truth and spoke about the real issues." The American people want the right things, but they have to come in the right package. Meanwhile, they will allow cymbals and gongs and loud singing to distract them, and the politicians will be happy to accommodate them.

After the Civil War was over, General Lee offered his sword to Grant at Appomattox and Grant turned it down. Then Lee asked Grant for two things. Number one, he was fearful he was going to be executed for treason and he asked Grant to help defend him, and Grant assured him he would do everything he could to make sure that did not happen. Then Lee asked

Grant if his men could have their horses; it was planting time and they were not going to be able to make a crop without their horses. If they could not make a crop, they would starve during the next winter. Grant also agreed to that request.

Then Lee, accompanied by four or five aides, got on his beautiful horse, Traveler, and started the seven-day trip to Richmond, where a home had been prepared for him. Lee was a remarkable man. He had not wanted Virginia to secede, had not wanted the South to secede, and had thought the war unnecessary. Nevertheless, he could not persuade his beloved Virginia. About the third day out of Appomattox on that trip, he came to a place where everything had been leveled. Everything was burned, rotting corpses were in the fields, and there was total destruction. He got off Traveler, turned to one of his aides, and with a wave of the hand said, "You know, the politicians caused this. At a time when the country needed men of intelligence, courage, and forebearance, all we got were politicians feeding our bigotries and our hostilities and our prejudices until this war became inevitable."

Conclusion

The political system created by our great Constitution has served us well. We need leaders of intelligence who have courage, integrity, concern for the downtrodden, and a passion for peace and justice. With such leaders, there is no problem we cannot solve.

THE RELIGION CLAUSES
OF THE FIRST AMENDMENT IN
HISTORICAL PERSPECTIVE

by

Harold J. Berman

Harold J. Berman

Harold J. Berman is Woodruff Professor of Law at Emory University. He is also James Barr Ames Professor of Law Emeritus at Harvard University, where he taught from 1948 to 1985. His courses include Comparison of Soviet and American Law, the Western Legal Tradition, and the Law of International Trade.

Professor Berman is the author of twenty books, including Law and Revolution: The Formation of the Western Legal Tradition *(1983),* Justice in the U.S.S.R. *(Revised edition, 1963), and* The Interaction of Law and Religion *(1974), and more than 200 articles.*

He has written and lectured widely on comparative law, legal history, and legal philosophy generally, as well as on Soviet affairs and on trade between Communist and non-Communist countries.

Professor Berman has been active in promoting the teaching of law in the liberal arts curriculum. His book The Nature and Functions of Law: An Introduction for Students of the Arts and Sciences *(1958; 4th ed., 1980, with William R. Greiner) is widely used in college courses. He is also editor and co-author of* Talks on American Law *(2nd ed., 1971).*

He is co-founder and member of the Editorial Board of the Journal of Law and Religion *and has served on the Board of Directors of the Council on Religion and Law since its formation in 1975.*

Born in 1918 in Hartford, Connecticut, Professor Berman received the B.A. degree from Dartmouth College in 1938. He studied at the London School of Economics and Political Science in 1938-39 and at Yale Graduate School and Yale Law School. He received the M.A. (1942) and the LL.B. (1947) from Yale University. He taught law at Stanford University in 1947-48. He served in the United States Army in the European Theatre of Operations from 1942 to 1945, and received the Bronze Star Medal.

THE RELIGION CLAUSES OF THE FIRST AMENDMENT IN HISTORICAL PERSPECTIVE

by

Harold J. Berman

In this lecture I shall first trace in broad outline the historical evolution of the relationship between the Christian church and what we loosely call the state, that is, political authority, from the beginnings of Christianity until the adoption of the Constitution of the United States so that we may better understand the historical significance of the Religion Clauses of the First Amendment from the perspective of those who framed and adopted them. Second, I shall examine the subsequent development of that relationship in the nineteenth and twentieth centuries so that we may better understand the historical significance of the Religion Clauses of the First Amendment from the perspective of where we are today.

Needless to say, to attempt such a portrayal in a few pages will require a very broad brush, and the result will be only a very rough sketch. You may well ask, Why do this? My answer is twofold: First, we need to be reminded that the authors of the United States Constitution—and here I include not only those who drafted it but also those who ratified it—fully recognized that they were taking a giant step forward in the history of mankind. In the words of the seal of the new republic, words which are today reproduced on the reverse side of every one-dollar bill, they proclaimed a *novus ordo saeclorum*, a "new order of the ages." I should like to retell in a few words the earlier history of church-state relations as those men understood that history, in the hope of recapturing some neglected but important aspects of the meaning which they attributed to the extraordinary changes that they attempted to effectuate.

Second, we need to understand how far we have become removed, during the past seventy-five years, from that earlier history to which the framers were responding and against which they were reacting. The "new order of the ages" into which they entered—which, indeed, they helped to create—is vastly different from the new historical era into which we have entered in the past two generations since the outbreak of the First World War. We cannot possibly return to the situation of the Founding Fathers. Yet at the same time, it would be folly simply to reject what they achieved. We must, on the contrary, build on their accomplishments. We must ourselves be guided by the experience of the past, as they were, in our search for new solutions to the tensions between religion and government that confront us as we enter yet another "new order of the ages."

I

"The people of the United States of America," as they officially called themselves for the first time in 1789, looked back on five eras of the history of the Christian church in its relationship to political authority.

In the first era, the highest political authority of the Roman Empire outlawed Christian worship. This was, from the Christian point of view, separation of church and state with a vengeance. From the imperial point of view, however, it was the union of religion and government, since the emperor was himself considered to be divine and since pagan cult worship was an integral part of imperial law.

In the second era, starting in the fourth century A.D., Christianity was established as the official religion of the Empire. The emperor lost his divinity. He became, however, the head of the church, who convoked and himself presided over church councils, appointed and removed patriarchs and bishops, and founded and administered monasteries. "I am emperor and I am priest," declared the Byzantine Emperor Constantine. At a later time this system of imperial dominion within the church was called "caesaropapism."

The same system prevailed also in the West. Before their conversion to Christianity in the late fifth to eighth centuries, the Germanic kings, like the pagan Roman emperors, were considered to be divine and were the cult leaders, as well as the military leaders, of their people. Upon conversion they, too, lost their divinity yet continued as sacral rulers of the church within their respective territories. They invested the clergy in their spiritual offices and were overlords of the church property which the clergy administered. Even the bishop of Rome, who by tradition was the most prestigious and the most independent of the higher clergy in the West, and whose consecration was welcomed by the Frankish emperors of the eighth

to early eleventh centuries, was at the same time
almost wholly under their political, economic, and
sometimes even spiritual domination.

A third era in the history of the interrelationship of
ecclesiastical and secular authorities was introduced
in the century between 1050 and 1150, when a large
part of the clergy throughout Western Christendom
united under the bishop of Rome to form an independent polity, separate from the secular authority
of emperors, kings, and feudal lords. This was the
Papal Revolution, which broke into violence in the Investiture Controversy of 1075 – 1122. In 1075, in his
famous *Dictates of the Pope*, Gregory VII proclaimed
that emperors and kings had no authority over the
church; that the bishop of Rome alone had authority
to ordain, discipline, depose, and reinstate bishops,
to convoke and control councils, and to establish and
administer abbeys and bishoprics; that only the pope
had authority "to enact new laws according to the
needs of the time"; that the papal court was "the court
of the whole of Christendom," to which all Christians
had a right to resort in matters within the ecclesiastical jurisdiction; and, indeed, that the pope "may
depose emperors" and "is the only one whose feet are
to be kissed by all princes."

Under Pope Gregory VII and his successors, the
Roman Catholic Church established itself as a unified,
hierarchical, independent, political-legal entity. By
the Concordat of Worms of 1122, the secular power
lost its right to invest priests and bishops with the
symbols of their offices. The church also asserted its
own independent property rights in the vast ecclesias-

tical holdings which constituted nearly one-third of the land of Western Europe.

Thus a dual system of government was introduced: Both secular and ecclesiastical authorities ruled in the same territories and over the same people, with overlapping jurisdictions. The secular state raised armies, controlled violence, taxed, regulated commerce, and governed property relations, and in so doing it inevitably exercised large powers not only over the laity but also over the clergy. The ecclesiastical state governed most aspects of the life of the clergy (including their commercial and property relations with each other) and also largely controlled the religious, family, moral, and ideological aspects of the life of the laity.

This was, indeed, for the first time in the history of Christianity, and perhaps for the first time in the history of mankind, a genuine separation of church and state, in the sense that the church was independent of the state—or, more precisely, the all-Western church-state was independent of the various Western secular states—in regulating what were denominated as spiritual matters, while the secular states were independent of the church in regulating what were denominated as temporal matters. Yet the division between what was considered spiritual and what was considered temporal remained a matter of recurrent tension and dispute, requiring extraordinary measures of cooperation and competition between the two concurrent jurisdictions. For example, both pope and emperor, or pope and king, had to agree on the appointment of archbishops and bishops, and when in 1208 King John of England would not

accept the pope's nominee as Archbishop of Canter-
bury, the pope placed the entire nation of England
under interdict, forbidding priests to perform marriages and burials and excommunicating and threatening to depose the king and to give his crown to the
King of France. After five years King John capitu-
lated, surrendering England to the pope as a fief,
swearing an oath of vassalage, and agreeing to send a
yearly tribute to Rome—which tribute, incidentally,
was paid annually for over three hundred years, until
Henry VIII replaced the pope as head of the English
Church. But even on a much lower level, in matters
of local government, in family matters, in property
matters, and generally in matters of civil and criminal
responsibility, church and state formed separate
cooperating and competing polities, separate cooperating and competing political and legal hierarchies, and
separate cooperating and competing lawmaking
bodies, within the same national or regional or urban
or village communities throughout Europe.

In the sixteenth century the very concept of a
visible, hierarchical, corporate church exercising a
political and legal jurisdiction came under attack.
Martin Luther, with the support, ultimately, of most
of the German princes, introduced a fourth era in the
history of "church and state." Theologically, Luther
replaced the Gregorian "two swords" theory with a
new theory of two kingdoms, the earthly and the
heavenly or, as he also put it, the kingdom of Law and
the kingdom of Gospel. The true church, he declared,
is the invisible community of faithful believers
established by the Gospel as part of the heavenly

kingdom. In the earthly kingdom, the church, to be sure, assumes a visible form; nevertheless, it retains its divine government in which all are priests, accountable for the spiritual welfare of each other. Therefore, the church needs no clerical hierarchy to mediate between God and the laity, no canon law to define the various paths for salvation, and no ecclesiastical courts to adjudicate disputes or punish wrongdoers. Every individual stands directly before God, is justified by faith alone, and is spared divine sanction only by God's grace.

Politically, Luther's radical separation of the earthly and heavenly kingdoms left all state authority to the civil ruler, the prince. This included political authority over the visible church itself, in its external life. The Christian prince was called both to establish and to protect the church within his domain, to help define its doctrine and liturgy, to discipline wicked preaching and maladministration of the sacraments, and to aid in the church's care for the poor, in its program of religious education, and in its efforts to achieve the moral improvement of society.

In Germany, the conflict between the Lutheran and the Roman Catholic parties was resolved in 1555 in the Religious Peace of Augsburg, which empowered each prince to establish either Catholicism or Lutheranism within his territory, under the principle *cuius regio eius religio* ("the ruler's religion shall prevail in his territory"). The prince was to govern the territorial church but had to permit dissenting Christian subjects to emigrate. In the imperial cities, on the other hand, Catholics and Lutherans were to have

equal rights. Non-Lutheran Protestants, however, such as Calvinists and the Anabaptists, were
outlawed.

In some ways the Lutheran Reformation represented
a return to the pre-twelfth-century system in which
the church had been an invisible community of
believers coextensive with the secular polity. But
Luther did not propose to restore the sacral kingship
or the priestly character of royal rule. And in
Germany the Lutheran Reformation resulted in
something quite different from caesaropapism, since
Germany was a confederation of many principalities
and, in addition, in each of those principalities the
powers of the ruler were limited by law. Absolute
monarchy—though always a threat—was a later development in Europe. The Roman Catholic principle
of the rule of law, which had previously rested on the
cooperation and competition of plural jurisdictions
within the same community, was preserved in the
new concept of a Christian monarchy which, though
omnicompetent, was limited by the twin doctrines of
the Christian calling of the monarch and the Christian
conscience of the faithful. Yet this new concept was
always in danger as long as the monarchy controlled
both ecclesiastical and secular affairs.

That danger was realized in the English Reforma-
tion of the sixteenth century, which was quite dif-
ferent in many respects from the German Reforma-
tion. England remained Catholic, though not Roman.
In 1534 the Supremacy Act declared that "the King's
Majesty justly and rightly is . . . the only Supreme
Head in Earth of the Church of England called the
Anglicana Ecclesia." Thus Henry VIII became both

king and pope, wielding both the temporal and the spiritual swords. He and his successors, through their parliaments, established a uniform liturgy, doctrine, and administration of the sacraments. Contraventions of royal religious policy were made punishable as treason. Not only Roman Catholics but also Lutherans, Calvinists, and Anabaptists were subjected to severe repression. In the early seventeenth century the Stuart kings expressly declared that their power was absolute, that is, that they were absolved from obedience to the law.

Yet this, too, was not, or at least not quite, caesaropapism. The monarchs, as laymen, could exercise no sacerdotal functions. Moreover, their rule of the church was also somewhat limited by parliamentary resistance to excessive royal intervention. Although parliaments could be convened only by royal authority and were subject to royal control, the growing Puritan faction within them helped to prevent the monarch from seizing too great a spiritual power and requiring too narrow a doctrine and liturgy. The Tudor and Stuart kings could repress but they could not extirpate the Roman Catholics on the right and the Puritans on the left. Thus pluralism remained, and, in addition, there remained among the judges, at least, the older tradition of the rule of law.

Eventually the Puritan Revolution of 1640 to 1660, the Restoration of 1660 to 1688, and the Glorious Revolution of 1688 – 1689 introduced a new era in the interrelationships of church and state: Parliament replaced the king as head of both church and state, and the Anglican Church remained the established church, but Parliament accepted as a constitutional

principle the toleration of the so-called dissenting
Protestant sects. This inaugurated a fifth stage in the
history of the relationship of ecclesiastical and secular
authority. In the Bill of Rights and the Toleration Act
of 1689, Parliament granted freedom of association
and worship to all Protestants. Many of the remaining
legal restrictions on the civil and political liberties of
Protestants were removed in the following decades.
Roman Catholicism, however, continued to be pro-
scribed by penal law. Jews, expelled from England
in the twelfth century, were readmitted in the
seventeenth by Cromwell's Puritan government; they
also were "tolerated" but remained under severe dis-
abilities.

At the time of the American Revolution, then, the
colonists could look back on a historical succession of
five different regimes of church-state relationships,
starting with (1) early Christianity, when the primitive
church defied the pagan state, followed by (2) the
Byzantine and Germanic regimes of unity of church
and state under a common imperial or royal sacral
ruler, and then in the eleventh and twelfth centuries
by (3) the Roman Catholic separation of the church,
now itself an ecclesiastical state, from imperial and
royal political authorities, which, by virtue of that
very separation became the first secular states in the
modern sense. In the sixteenth century there came
(4) the Lutheran break with Rome, resulting in
established churches within the various secular
principalities and kingdoms of Europe, culminating,
finally, in the seventeenth century, especially in
England, in a regime of (5) toleration of dissenting

Protestant sects within the system of an established church.

In colonial America, the principle of an established church (whether Anglican or Puritan), plus limited toleration of certain other churches, was accepted in many of the colonies. On the other hand, Rhode Island and Pennsylvania had no established church from the very beginning and extended toleration to Roman Catholics as well as to Jews. Indeed, in Providence Roger Williams proclaimed that there should be not only toleration but "free exercise of religion" and "pure liberty of conscience."

II

It was against this historical background that the Founders of the American republic introduced a new principle of church-state relations. The first formal step in its introduction was the decision made in 1791, in the First Amendment of the United States Constitution, to prohibit the federal government from establishing a religion or otherwise restricting the exercise by any person of his or her religious convictions. This left the regulation of church-state relationships almost entirely to the several states. At the same time, the Religion Clauses of the First Amendment exerted a powerful moral influence on those states that had established churches to disestablish them—which, indeed, over the next four decades, they did. Thus the earlier English principle of establishment with limited toleration was transformed into a principle of neutrality with respect to all

Protestant Christian denominations and a modified
neutrality with respect to Roman Catholics, Jews,
Muslims, and others. The United States Constitution
provided that no religious test may be required for
eligibility to a federal office, and the constitutions of
at least four states contained analogous provisions.

An establishment remained, nevertheless, both at
the state and at the federal level—not an establishment of any denomination but an establishment of
religion, and not an establishment of just any religion
but an establishment of a generalized Protestant
Christianity.

Let me give some examples:

In New York in 1811 the highest state court upheld
an indictment for blasphemous utterances against
Christ. Speaking for the court, Chief Justice Kent
stated that "we are a christian people, and the
morality of the country is deeply ingrafted upon christianity. . . ." The New York State Convention of 1821
endorsed the decision in that case, declaring that the
court was right in holding that the Christian religion
is the law of the land and to be preferred over all
other religions. These statements were confirmed in
an 1861 New York case in which the court said:

> "Religious tolerance is entirely consistent with a
> recognized religion. Christianity may be conceded
> to be the established religion, to the qualified ex-
> tent mentioned, while perfect civil and political
> equality, with freedom of conscience and religious
> preference, is secured to individuals of every
> other creed and profession."

Similarly, in Pennsylvania in 1822 a man was convicted of blasphemy for saying that "the Holy Scriptures were a mere fable" and that "they contained a great many lies." The Supreme Court of Pennsylvania, in affirming the conviction, stated:

> "Christianity, general Christianity, is and always has been a part of the common law of Pennsylvania; . . . not Christianity founded on any particular religious tenets; not Christianity with an established church, and tithes and spiritual courts; but Christianity with liberty of conscience to all men."

On the same grounds, laws restricting commercial activities on Sundays were upheld by courts of many states. In one such case Judge Scott, speaking for the Supreme Court of Missouri, stated:

> "Those who question the constitutionality of our Sunday laws seem to imagine that the [Missouri] constitution is to be regarded as an instrument framed for a state composed of strangers collected from all quarters of the globe, each with a religion of his own, bound by no previous social ties, nor sympathizing in any common reminiscences of the past; . . . [S]uch is not the mode by which our organic law is to be interpreted. We must regard the people for whom it was ordained. It appears to have been made by Christian men. The constitution, on its face, shows that the Christian religion was the religion of its framers." (*State v. Ambs*, 20 Mo. 214, 216–217 [1854].)

Similar judicial statements may be found in other states in similar cases involving blasphemy, violations of Sunday laws, and other religious offenses—notwithstanding the fact that the constitutions of virtually all the states contained provisions proclaiming religious liberty.

In addition, states did not hesitate to require the teaching of the Christian religion in prisons, reformatories, orphanages, homes for soldiers, and asylums. State colleges and universities as well as elementary and secondary schools required the reading of the Protestant Bible, the singing of Protestant hymns, and the saying of Protestant prayers.

These practices and these views prevailed well into the twentieth century.

Not only at the state levels but also at the federal level, it was generally assumed that America is a Christian country, and more particularly a Protestant Christian country, and that the First Amendment was intended to protect Christianity by freeing it from any governmental interference on the federal level and by giving all denominations equality before the law. The notion of a "wall of separation" which would prevent any government support of religion was alien to the realities of American constitutional law in the late eigthteenth, the nineteenth, and the early twentieth centuries. As Joseph Story wrote of the First Amendment in 1833:

"Probably at the time of the adoption of the Constitution, and of the [First Amendment], the general if not the universal sentiment in America was, that Christianity ought to receive encouragement from the State so far as was not incompatible with the private rights of conscience and the freedom of religious worship. An attempt to level all religions, and to make it a matter of state policy to hold all in utter indifference, would have created universal disapprobation, if not universal indignation. . . .

"The real object of the [First] [A]mendment was not to countenance, much less to advance, Mahometanism, or Judaism, or infidelity, by prostrating Christianity; but to exclude all rivalry among Christian sects, and to prevent any national ecclesiastical establishment which should give to a hierarchy the exclusive patronage of the national government. It thus cut off the means of religious persecution (the vice and pest of former ages), and of the subversion of the rights of conscience in matters of religion, which had been trampled upon almost from the days of the Apostles to the present age."

From the Constitutional Convention itself, in which Benjamin Franklin proposed that the delegates should resort to common prayer to break through an impasse in its deliberations; from the explicitly religious Presidential Proclamations of Washington, Adams, and Madison; from the designation of Christian chaplains for the army and navy and for the U.S. Congress itself; from the Northwest Ordinance of 1787 with its provisions for religious education; from federal support of Christian education of Indians, including Jefferson's own treaty with the Kaskasia Indians providing for a salary to be paid by the United

States Government for a Catholic priest and for
United States funding of the erection of a Catholic
church (the Kaskasia Indians having been converted
to Roman Catholicism); from exemption of religious
activities from federal taxation; and from a host of
other similar circumstances—it must be concluded
that the Establishment Clause of the First Amendment, drafted not by the Deist Jefferson but by the
Protestant Christian James Madison, was not intended to prevent any government aid to religion but
was intended rather to prevent the establishment of a
national religion.

Even Thomas Jefferson, though he was against
organized religion, believed firmly in "nature's God,"
"the Creator," the "Supreme Judge of the world"—all
terms to be found in the Declaration of Independence. In a Thanksgiving Proclamation issued
in 1797 when he was Governor of Virginia, Jefferson
appointed

> "a day of public and solemn thanksgiving and
> prayer to Almighty God, earnestly recommending
> to all the good people of this commonwealth, to set
> apart the said day for those purposes, and . . . the
> several ministers of religion to meet their respec-
> tive societies thereon . . . and generally to perform
> the sacred duties of their function, proper for the
> occasion."

Jefferson also believed that all religions share a
common morality which is essential to the welfare of
any society and that, more specifically, America
needed religion to give it the necessary inner strength

to survive. The First Amendment, Jefferson said, was an "experiment," designed to test whether religion could flourish in America without government support. He was confident that it could and that its ability to do so was essential to the maintenance of peace and order.

In contrast to Jefferson, James Madison derived the principle of religious liberty not primarily from its political utility in a pluralist society but also, and more immediately, from God's own will. In attacking proposed legislation in the 1780s in the State of Virginia that would have levied taxes to contribute (among other things) to the salaries of ministers, Madison stated that it is God who forbids the establishment of religion; that God wants men to worship him freely, not by coercion; and that this divine requirement transcends all political considerations. The covenant between God and man, Madison said, requires free exercise of religion, and that covenant takes precedence—"both in order of time and degree of obligation"—over the social contract. This statement of Madison makes implicit reference to the Lutheran doctrine of two kingdoms—the heavenly kingdom of grace and the earthly kingdom of law—as well as to the Calvinist doctrine of two covenants, one between God and man, the other between government and people. For Madison, the nonbeliever was in effect a third-party beneficiary of the divine covenant.

In stressing the importance of Christian concepts and values in the final achievement of religious freedom in America, I do not want to underestimate the importance also of Enlightenment concepts of

rationalism and individualism. It was the combination
of the two—Christian faith, strongly influenced by
Calvinist theology, and Deist skepticism, with its
strong antiecclesiastical tendency—that eventually
prevailed. The Religion Clauses of the First Amendment owe at least as much to Jonathan Edwards as to
Thomas Jefferson. Also, the struggle of the various
sects—especially the Baptists, the Quakers, and the
Congregationalists—against repression by one denomination or another was a decisive factor in bring-
ing about what may be called a Christian pluralism.
Madison supplemented his theological argument with
an ecclesiastical one: that the "multiplicity of sects,
which pervades America, . . . is the best and only
security for religious belief in any society." This position was not grounded solely in pragmatism; it was
grounded also, and primarily, in principle: the
principle that religion itself—religious belief—
depends for its validity on the freedom to disbelieve.

III

Within the past two generations the people of the
United States have entered into a new, seventh era in
the historical development of the interrelationship
between religion and government. The public philosophy of America has shifted radically from a religious
to a secular theory of the state, from a moral to a
political or instrumental theory, and from a communi-
tarian to an individualistic theory. Government and
law are now generally considered—at least in public
discourse—to be essentially a pragmatic device for
accomplishing specific political, economic, and social

objectives. Their tasks are thought to be finite, material, impersonal—to get things done, to make people act in certain ways. Rarely, if ever, does one hear it said that government and law are a reflection of an objective justice or of the ultimate meaning or purpose of life. Usually they are thought to reflect, at best, the community's sense of what is useful.

Likewise, it is only in the last two generations that the concept of religion as something wholly private and wholly psychological, as contrasted with the earlier concept of religion as something public, something partly psychological but also partly social and historical, indeed, partly political and legal, has come to dominate our discourse.

These contemporary views of religion and government are supported by the Enlightenment philosophy of the late eighteenth century, with its emphasis on rationalism and individualism, and its attempt to divorce law and morality from religious faith—the sense of the just from the sense of the holy. The Puritan Christian tradition has been excluded from our public discourse. It is no accident that in recent decades our courts and writers have so often cited Thomas Jefferson, America's leading apostle of the Enlightenment, when they interpret the Religion Clauses of the First Amendment in such a way as to separate entirely the sphere of government from the sphere of belief.

In reacting against these contemporary views, many Americans, including some Justices of the United States Supreme Court, would turn the clock back to the founding period. Chief Justice Rehnquist, for example, contends, in effect, that since the

Religion Clauses were not originally intended to be applied to the states, they should be restricted—as they were until the 1940s—to federal legislative, executive, and judicial action involving religion. He contends, further, that if the Religion Clauses are to be applied to state legislative, executive, and judicial action, then they should be interpreted to mean what they were understood to mean in 1791: More especially, "establishment" should be understood to mean not state "aid" to religion but rather state endorsement of a religious creed.

There are, in my view, at least two strong objections to that solution. First, it would be a sign not of respect but of disrespect for constitutional history for the courts to overrule the precedents of the past forty-five years in favor of precedents of a more distant time. Our constitutional history is an ongoing history. It is a living tradition, not a mere historicism. Jaroslav Pelikan has defined tradition as the living faith of the dead, traditionalism as the dead faith of the living. It is an example of traditionalism, not tradition—of historicism, not a belief in history—to try to restore the original understanding of the First Amendment.

Second, the religious context of the First Amendment as originally understood—and as understood at least until World War I—no longer exists, and the public philosophy generated in that context no longer exists. Today we are groping for a new public philosophy—one that will build on the past but will not be bound by the past. Such a public philosophy must be grounded in something more than the practical need to maintain peace among warring factions. It must look beyond our pluralism to the common convictions that underlie our pluralism. It must come to grips with the fact that freedom of belief—which includes freedom of disbelief—rests, in the last analysis, on the foundation of belief, not on the foundation of skepticism. That is what John Adams meant when he said that the Constitution, with its guarantee of freedom to believe or disbelieve, "was made only for a moral and religious people. It will be wholly inadequate to any other." It is not to be regarded as an instrument framed (in Judge Scott's words) for a society "composed of strangers . . . each with a religion of his own, bound by no previous social ties, not sympathizing in any common reminiscences of the past."

At the same time—and here I speak in the spirit more of the last two generations than of the first two-and-one-half centuries of our history as a nation—our public philosophy must also come to grips with the deep conflict in our society between orthodox religious belief systems and widespread indifference or opposition to such belief systems. We have in the past sought to resolve this conflict largely by trying to sweep it under the rug. We have pretended that all belief, both religious and nonreligious, is the private affair of each individual. Public figures and others who participate in shaping public opinion have for the most part been unwilling to express publicly—that is, outside their own like-minded groups—their deepest convictions concerning religious questions. When they have done so, they have been attacked as overstepping the bounds of public discourse. This has inhibited the articulation of a public philosophy

grounded in our fundamental beliefs concerning human nature, human destiny, and the sources and
limits of human knowledge.

IV

If public discourse concerning the interrelationship
of religion and government in the United States today
is to make sense, we must recognize that each of the
six historical eras which we have experienced in the
past two millennia has left an important legacy. We
remain heirs to those Christians and Jews who defied
the unjust laws of the pagan Roman emperors and
who practiced their divine duty of civil disobedience.
Martin Luther King belongs in their ranks. We
remain heirs also to the sacral emperors and kings in
both Eastern and Western Christendom from the
fourth and fifth to the eleventh centuries who were
not only the political and military rulers of their
peoples but also their religious rulers. To be sure,
they abused their office; yet they can teach us,
whether by positive or negative example, that, in the
words of Alexis de Tocqueville a century and a half
ago, "It is only by scrupulous conformity to religious
morality in great affairs that [those who govern] can
hope to teach the community at large to know, to
love, and to observe it in the lesser concerns of life."
(*Democracy in America*, Vol. II, Vintage Books, 1945,
p. 156.) For better or worse, we expect our president
to be a spiritual and not only a political leader. We
remain heirs also to the third era of church-state
relations, from the twelfth to the sixteenth century,
when the visible corporate church stood opposite the

secular royal and feudal powers and sought to hold
them to higher standards—and to the fourth era as
well, when the invisible priesthood of all believers
held up to their princely rulers the doctrines of the
Christian calling and of Christian conscience. Nor can
we denounce the heritage of the fifth era of limited
toleration within a system of an established Anglican
church, or of the sixth era of unlimited toleration
within a system of an established Protestant Christianity. We owe our Constitution not only to the last of
these eras but to all six of them, for although each
rebelled against its predecessor, each was part of the
entire succession.

In each of these eras it was presupposed that both
religion and government were essential to the preservation and development of a healthy social order. In
each it was also presupposed that religion and government were interconnected. Even where, as in the
United States, it was generally accepted that church
and state were to be free from each other's control, it
was also generally accepted that religion and government must—and should—have a reciprocal influence
upon each other. On the one hand, officeholders were
not expected to shed their religious commitments at
the door of the office. On the other hand, religious
leaders were to play a constructive part in the political
life of the country. "The separation of church and
state" was never understood to exclude the cooperation of religion and government.

What distinguishes most sharply our situation in
the latter half of the twentieth century from that of
previous centuries is the fact that in our public discourse separation of church and state has come to

mean separation of religion and government, and this in turn has stripped much of our political discourse of its religious dimension at the same time that it has stripped much of our religious discourse of its political dimension.

At the outset of this essay I said that we cannot return to the situation of the Founding Fathers or even to that of our own greatgrandparents, but that nevertheless we should be guided by the experience of the past in our search for solutions to the tensions between religion and government that confront us as we enter a new age. My conclusions are, first, that there should be open discussion of the historical roots of the Religion Clauses of the First Amendment, and particularly their roots in the religious convictions of the people who framed and ratified them; and, second, that we should seek new ways in which government and religion can cooperate with each other without either an establishment of religion or a prohibition of its free exercise.

Such cooperation would require that we give a somewhat broader meaning to the term "religion" than that which has prevailed in recent decades in the application of the Establishment Clause and a somewhat narrower meaning to the term "establishment." That would have the effect of permitting government support of theistic and deistic belief systems more nearly comparable to the government support which is permitted to be given to agnostic and atheist belief systems. It would also help to correct the present situation in which citizens are encouraged publicly to advance what are considered to be rational, secular arguments for political action but are discouraged from publicly advancing what are considered to be nonrational religious arguments. Such a shift toward what has been called the "accommodation" of religion by government would, I submit, help to reconcile the experience of the past two generations with that of the past two millennia of our history.

THE ACCOMMODATION OF
RELIGIOUS CONSCIENCE

by

Christopher F. Mooney, S.J.

Christopher F. Mooney, S.J.

Christopher F. Mooney was born in Bayonne, New Jersey, in 1925. He completed his undergraduate studies in classics at Loyola University, Chicago, and became a member of the Society of Jesus. He received his master's degree in history from Loyola University and pursued theological studies at Woodstock College, where he was ordained priest in 1957. His doctoral studies in theology were made at the Catholic University of Paris, after which he was appointed to the Theology Department at Fordham University in 1964, specializing in the area of religion and society. In 1965 he became Chair of the Deparment, and served in that capacity until 1969, when he was chosen President of Woodstock College. After five years at Woodstock, he spent a year as graduate fellow at Yale Law School, earning the degree of Master of Studies in Law in 1975. The summer of 1977 was spent on the staff of the General Counsel of the U.S. Commission on Civil Rights. In 1978 he received the Juris Doctor degree from the University of Pennsylvania and was admitted to the Pennsylvania Bar. He then served for two years as Assistant Dean of the University of Pennsylvania Law School before coming to Fairfield University, where he was Academic Vice President from 1980 to 1987. He is now Professor of Religious Studies at Fairfield.

In 1966 Harper and Row published his first book, Teilhard de Chardin and the Mystery of Christ, *which won the National Catholic Book Award, and was later translated into Spanish and French. Later books include* The Making of Man *(1971),* Man Without Tears *(1975),* Religion and the American Dream *(1977), and* Inequality and the American Conscience *(1982). His most recent work,* Public Virtue: Law and the Social Character of Religion, *published by the University of Notre Dame Press in 1986, won the Alpha Sigma Nu Award in the Humanities.*

Fr. Mooney is a member of the National Association of College and University Attorneys, the American Bar Association and the American Legal Studies Association. He has served on the executive council of the Society for the Scientific Study of Religion and is a member of the Catholic Theological Society of America, the American Academy of Religion, and the Council on Religion and Law.

THE ACCOMMODATION
OF RELIGIOUS CONSCIENCE

by

Christopher F. Mooney, S. J.

The Supreme Court has made a very special effort
over the years to spell out the meaning of our nation's
First Amendment commitment to religious freedom.
The Justices have tended to focus upon the protection
of the individual's right to act in conscience on the
basis of his or her most deeply held beliefs. The
religion clauses guarantee that such freedom of conscience is privileged and that its exercise is not only to
be encouraged, but may even be positively promoted
by government. Exemption for the conscientious
objector to all war is but one example of such government "benevolence" toward religious freedom, an
accommodation of Congress's power to raise armies
with its recognition of the importance of free exercise
values.

Yet the dilemma which the nation has faced since
the founding of the republic is how to reconcile this
ideal of benevolence toward the free exercise of
religion with that other ideal we have always aspired
to, namely that of disestablishment, the neutrality of
government toward religion, its separation from and
noninvolvement in religious matters. The force of this
dilemma was caught in 1963 by Justice Brennan when
he observed, in a concurring opinion, "[H]ow elusive

is the line which enforces the Amendment's injunction of strict neutrality, while maintaining no hostility toward religion." (*Abington School District v. Schempp*, 374 U.S. 203, 231 [1963].) How are we as a nation to locate this line between benevolence toward religious freedom, which is permissible, and the advancement of religion by government, which is not? How are we to know whether an action is in fact neutral toward religion and constitutes neither interference nor sponsorship?

The first step in answering these questions is to know what the Founders thought about their nascent government's relation to religion. My starting point will therefore be to ask how the Founders went about constructing a secular federal government in an essentially religious society. I then want to take a present-day case study: the current legal challenges of fundamentalist Christians to what they feel to be threats to their religious values in the nation's public schools. How have the courts reacted to these claims of conscience? Finally, I want to discuss two problem areas in the interrelationship of religion and government where in the future a willingness for compromise is both desirable and possible. In the first area such willingness will be required on the part of many religious people, who will have to accommodate their consciences to the legal restrictions established by the Supreme Court. In the second area such willingness will be required on the part of the Supreme Court itself. There will thus be four parts to my approach to this problem of religious conscience.

I

How did the Founders think about government's relation to religion? To seek an answer to this question is to unravel the extraordinary complexity and variety in the ways religion was regarded at the time of the Revolution and during the years immediately preceding the Constitution of 1787. It is also to expose the multiple and finally unsolvable ambiguities connected with the wording of the First Amendment. The thoughts of Jefferson and Madison are most often cited to explain the intent of the religion clauses. (The Supreme Court, in its early decisions on government and religion, repeatedly refers to these two statesmen.) But Jefferson had nothing at all to do with the clauses; he was not even in the country at the time the Constitution was debated or the Bill of Rights hammered out, and his famous "wall of separation" metaphor did not appear in his writings until more than a decade later. Madison was indeed a chief architect of both the Constitution and the Bill of Rights, but the language of the First Amendment, though certainly not uncongenial to him, was very possibly not his work at all. So we need to look more closely.

Bernard Bailyn has documented with admirable clarity what he calls the "contagion of liberty" that swept America and infected all areas of colonial life. Indeed, as he says, "the fear of a comprehensive conspiracy against liberty . . . lay at the heart of the Revolution." (Bailyn, *The Ideological Origins of the American Revolution*, Harvard University Press,

1967, p. ix.) It was therefore taken for granted that
the purpose of all constitutions in the colonies was to
specify and protect inalienable rights and to limit the
ordinary actions of government. The suspicion of
every type of political power not derived from the
people inevitably became a suspicion of ecclesiastical
power also, since that too represented a form of
coercion, the dominion of some people over others.

Only in the case of slavery did this challenge to
dominion falter for economic reasons and finally fail,
though even here the "contagion of liberty" exposed
the contradiction in all its ugliness and prompted
even statesmen from the southern colonies to look
forward to a time when "this lamentable evil" could
be abolished. Madison's sad words at the Constitutional Convention anticipated the arguments of
moderates a generation later: "Great as the evil is, a
dismemberment of the union would be worse."
(Quoted by Henry F. May, *The Enlightenment in
America,* Oxford University Press, 1976, p. 100.)
Churchly power, however, had no such economic
protection from the "logic of Revolutionary thought."
Bailyn notes how weak and ill defined were the
establishments in the various colonies; yet they came
under fire nevertheless, both from sectarians, who
wanted freedom *for* their sects, and from political
idealists, inspired by the rationalism of the Enlightenment, who wanted freedom *from* these same sects.

The sectarians, also referred to as dissenters, were
the Baptists, the largest in number and the most
vocal; the Quakers; and many Methodists and Presbyterians. They tended to see all government nega-
tively, as being mainly coercive in character, and

believed in the complete separation of religion as the highest manifestation of their liberty as Christians. The movement's early leaders, Roger Williams and William Penn, created in Rhode Island and Pennsylvania something totally new at the time, colonies without establishments. Later, when the Constitution was written, Baptist leaders like John Leland of Virginia and Isaac Backus of Massachusetts wanted freedom as a right, not as a favor from weak state establishments. Their movement's acute individualism and religious impluse of withdrawal accorded well with the civic individualism of the "enlightened," and it was, as Bailyn says, "touched by the magic of the Revolutionary thought" and transformed. (Bailyn, *op. cit.*, p. 271.)

Jefferson and Madison were both "enlightened," and as such viewed religion instrumentally, as very much a private affair of conscience and opinion, but something nevertheless very useful for the promotion of civic virtue. Jefferson believed that any truths about God and the universe could be known by rational examination of nature alone, without need of any divine revelation, and this conviction he distilled in what he regarded as second in his writings only to the Declaration of Independence, Virginia's Act for Establishing Religious Freedom. Madison, who was influenced by the Anglicanism of his youth and, as a student at Princeton, much more by the Presbyterianism of John Witherspoon, seems to have held beliefs more profound and complex than those of Jefferson and clearly not as opposed to the concept of revealed religion. Yet he was nevertheless an adamant foe of establishment. Faced with a 1785 proposal in

the Virginia House of Delegates for a threepence tax
to provide for religion teachers, he wrote his
"Memorial and Remonstrance Against Religious
Assessments," which gave his reason for this opposition: Establishment had meant coercion in the past,
and it was therefore a violation of basic human
freedom to require anyone to support a religious un-
dertaking.

The noninvolvement of government in religious
matters was, therefore, the principle defended by
Jefferson and Madison throughout their lives. This
they did primarily to protect freedom of conscience.
But they both also wanted to promote the freedom of
religious practice, in Jefferson's case because he saw
that such practice promoted good citizenship, in
Madison's case because he also saw it as a bulwark to
strengthen religious belief. Hence their principle of
separation was not an absolute, all-inclusive prohibition but could be accommodated on occasion to
advance political and perhaps also, for Madison,
religious ends.

As Governor of Virginia, Jefferson drafted a Bill for
Appointing Days of Public Fasting and Thanksgiving
(introduced by Madison in the Virginia legislature),
which required all ministers to preach on these
occasions, and he did not hesitate to invoke "nature's
God" in the Declaration of Independence and in his
second inaugural address as President. For his part,
Madison raised no constitutional objection in Congress, less than two months after the First Amendment became effective, to government support of a
chaplaincy system; and, as President during the War
of 1812, he issued four proclamations recommending

public days of prayer and fasting, though much later in his life he considered both actions to have been ill-advised.

This effort of Madison to avoid collisions in the religious area appears clearly in *The Federalist Papers*, where in Numbers 10 and 51 he captured perfectly that suspicion of power which, as we saw earlier, was the dominant political ethos of the time. He specifically mentions religion as one of the causes of competing "factions," groups seeking to advance their narrow private concerns. These factions, he says, are inevitable in a free government, and the aim of a separation of powers in the new Constitution should be not to harmonize but to neutralize them, thereby enabling enlightened elected leaders more easily to perceive and promote the common good. In Number 51, Madison finds in religion the analogy for this realistic pluralistic stance:

> "In a free government the security for civil rights must be the same as that for religious rights. It consists in the one case in the multiplicity of interests, and in the other in the multiplicity of sects. The degree of security in both cases will depend on the number of interests and sects."

It is scarcely possible to overestimate this combined influence of sectarians and the enlightened on the enactment of the religion clauses of the First Amendment. Nevertheless, five states still had establishments when the first Congress began discussing a bill of rights in 1789, and their representatives wanted nothing in the clauses which would jeopardize those establishments. To complicate matters more,

many delegates were Federalists, who, like Madison
himself, believed that the Constitution had no need
to provide for the protection of individual rights at all,
since these were already guaranteed by the fact that
actions of the Federal Government were limited to
what the Constitution explicitly allowed. Since the
Constitution granted no power over religion, all
religious matters were therefore reserved to the exclusive authority of the states.

Anti-federalists, on the other hand, believed that
powers already delegated by the Constitution might
be exercised by the Federal Government in ways, as
yet unspecified, that could restrict speech, establish
and aid religion, etc., unless the use of these powers
was curbed by explicit amendments. The Federalists
probably agreed to support such amendments in
order to get the Constitution ratified. Madison, in any
case, though opposed to a bill of rights in principle,
honored his own commitment by introducing in the
First Congress two separate amendments on religious
freedom. Both were firmly rooted in the theory of
religious pluralism that he had espoused in *The
Federalist Papers.*

The first of his proposed amendments was this:
"The civil rights of none shall be abridged on account
of religious belief or worship, nor shall any national
religion be established, nor shall the full and equal
rights of conscience be in any manner, or in any
pretext, infringed." The second read, "No State shall
violate the equal rights of conscience." Several objections were raised immediately to the effect that these
provisions might injure religion. Madison's reply
emphasized his double concern to prevent coercion

and to encourage a multiplicity of sects. He said that "he apprehended the meaning of the words to be, that Congress shall not establish a religion, and enforce the legal observation of it by law, nor compel men to worship God in any manner contrary to their conscience." He "believed that the people feared one sect might gain pre-eminence, or two combine together, and establish a religion to which they would compel others to conform."

After discussion and modification by two committees (Madison was a member of one), the amendments went to the full House. Samuel Livermore of New Hampshire moved the following: "Congress shall make no laws touching religion, or infringing the rights of conscience." This was again modified by a version proposed by Fisher Ames of Massachusetts, which the House finally adopted: "Congress shall make no law establishing religion, or to prevent the free exercise thereof, or to infringe the rights of conscience." The House also passed Madison's second amendment regarding the states. In the Senate this second amendment was immediately dropped, no doubt because of suspicion of federal power over the states, and the first House amendment was changed again: "Congress shall make no law establishing articles of faith or a mode of worship, or prohibiting the free exercise of religion." This revision was apparently not acceptable to the House, however. A conference committee of both houses, of which Madison was a member, then produced the final form that we have today: "Congress shall make no law respecting an establishment of religion, or prohibiting the free exercise thereof." (The texts are from the

Annals of the Congress of the United States, cited by
Michael J. Malbin, *Religion and Politics: The In-
tentions of the Authors of the First Amendment,*
American Enterprise Institute, 1978, pp. 6–14.)

We shall never know whether Madison actually
composed this final version, since the documentation
is so incomplete. The main issue, in any case, has
never been whether or not the words were his but
rather what they meant precisely. A heated debate in
recent years has come to focus on the establishment
clause. Is this the governing clause, with religious
freedom *defined* by the absolute character of the
separation? In other words, did the establishment
clause intend to restrict Congress from passing any
laws at all regarding religion (which seems to have
been Madison's principle), or did it really intend to
permit some form of government support for religion
as long as this did not prefer one religion to another?
The latter alternative would mean that free exercise,
not disestablishment, was the governing principle;
that Congress was being charged primarily with the
care of religious freedom; and that federal involvement in religious matters could be justified to
the extent that it promoted such freedom.

Each side of this debate has been trying to find
clues of exact intent through minute analyses of
whatever records survive. In the end, neither array of
arguments is wholly convincing, and the controversy
will very likely never be settled, simply because not
enough evidence exists and what does exist is
ambiguous on many points. The truth probably lies
somewhere in between. That is to say, the establishment clause did not necessarily mean the same thing

to all the framers. In regard to wording, for example, it is clear that it was not Madison but Ames and Livermore (both from states with establishments) who supplied the verbal core of both clauses. Madison said his most valuable proposal was the one prohibiting states from violating rights of conscience, but that proposal was rejected. Hence the clauses cannot be said to express his thought *tout court*.

On the other hand, the clauses clearly did not repudiate his views entirely or he would certainly have objected publicly. We must remember that, like all the other "enlightened," Madison believed that everything could be settled by compromise. Because he wanted agreement on the form of the Amendment, he very likely accepted phrasing he did not fully approve but finally could not change. On the Senate side the original wording indeed supports the position that the intent was no more than to prohibit the preference of one group over another. This version was not finally adopted, however, though the reasons for its rejection are not clear. Collectively, the majority of the Congress seems to have meant something more by nonestablishment than simply the safeguarding of religious freedom. But how much more?

This is precisely the question we cannot answer with any degree of certitude, although one action by this First Congress did indicate that "more" did not signify total noninvolvement of the Federal Government with things religious. The same legislators who enacted the First Amendment also, with no dissent from Madison, readopted in 1789 the Northwest Ordinance of 1787, first passed by the Continental

Congress, the third article of which read as follows: "Religion, morality and knowledge, being necessary to good government and the happiness of mankind, schools and the means of learning shall forever be encouraged." After citing this bit of evidence, Walter Berns pointedly remarks, "It is not easy to see how Congress, or a territorial government acting under the authority of Congress, could promote religious and moral education under a Constitution that . . . forbade all forms of assistance to religion." (Walter Berns, *The First Amendment and the Future of American Democracy,* Gateway Editions, 1985, p. 8.) Also, in the course of debating the First Amendment, the First Congress recommended a day of national thanksgiving and prayer. Encouragement of religion in general is evident, finally, in the fact that public taxes at the time were paying for military, legislative, and prison chaplains.

We must conclude, then, that we can know what the framers meant by the religion clauses only up to a point and not beyond. All of them, whether for religious or civic reasons, wanted the numerous religious bodies to flourish in society in complete freedom. All of them wanted to prohibit a *national* establishment of religion, while saying nothing about existing *state* establishments. All of them wanted to prohibit any intrusion by government into an in- dividual's freedom of conscience, whether this freedom be of a specifically religious nature or not. This broad consensus on general policy, however, was driven by large differences in motivation. To use John Courtney Murray's distinction (though not in a way he would have approved), for some framers the two clauses were simply "articles of peace," good and prudent lawmaking made socially necessary by the "contagion of liberty"; for others they were just as surely "articles of faith," either theological convictions that freedom from government was a religious imperative or Enlightenment ideologies that such freedom was a natural right.

As for Madison, he may well have wanted Congress to require a greater degree of separation than many members desired. The framers were certainly influenced by his convictions that religious freedom should be limited neither by religious institutions nor by government and that all such institutions should be denied the support of government power. But we cannot determine the degree of this influence. Too many minds and motives were at work; too many differences and ambiguities surfaced on secondary issues; too many compromises went into the vagueness and grand simplicity of the text.

II

This brief overview of the Founders' understanding of the religion clauses of the First Amendment puts us in a position now to take as a case study the current legal challenges brought by Christians of the fundamentalist movement, who feel their religious beliefs are threatened today by certain public school curricula. In his well-documented study of the movement, George Marsden explains that these fundamentalists are evangelicals in that revivalist tradition that dominated America for a large part of the nineteenth century. What set fundamentalism apart was its alarm over the early theological and cultural trends of this century and its sponsorship of a militant crusade against what was then called modernism and is now called secular humanism.

Like all other revivalists, fundamentalists believe in the absolute inerrancy of the Bible, the necessity of a conversion experience, and the importance of a holy life. Beginning in the 1950s the Moral Majority developed from this heritage and soon began to focus on secular humanism as a quasi-religious force threatening to displace Christianity entirely from the culture. Always alarmed at any moral decline they perceived, fundamentalists now developed a conspiracy theory which found secular humanism to be responsible not only for the moral pluralism in the country, but also for all recent decisions of the Supreme Court on religious questions. (George M. Marsden, *Fundamentalism and American Culture*, Oxford University Press, 1980.) Their response to moral ambiguity was to draw the sharpest distinction between good and evil, one that polarizes moral attitudes between satanic relativism and multiple stringent absolutes.

This dualistic revival continues unabated today, not only in its extreme form but also in more modest guises that appeal to large segments of middle America. The reason for this appeal is that most mainline religious people, while by disposition not militant at all, still believe that the Judaeo-Christian value system ought somehow to be privileged in this country. They have been encouraged in this belief by the religious rhetoric of high public officials, which touches such a responsive chord because it speaks to changes in the way society views sex, family life, and education.

Because there exists in the nation as a whole a longing for the moral certainties of the past, the majority of Americans are still looking for constants, beliefs they can rely on in the midst of accelerating change. Religion still makes a difference in their lives, and their fears are immediately aroused when they hear that it has been displaced by secularism. Why, they ask, should secularism become privileged in this country? If there is to be a disestablishment of religion, why should there be an establishment of irreligion? Why should the nonbeliever, whose freedom has been guaranteed by believers, suddenly become dominant, able coercively to exclude religion from the public sphere?

This general concern for moral values in the country received sharp focus from fundamentalists in 1987 through three legal challenges. All three dealt with religion in public schools, a not surprising fact since public schools are as close as we have come as a nation to a religious establishment. Two of these three challenges concerned elementary and secondary school textbooks. In Greenville, Tennessee, seven fundamentalist families initially won the right in federal district court to withdraw their children from reading classes and provide them with alternative instruction because they found that the Holt, Rhinehart & Winston basic reading series could cause a child to "adopt the view of a feminist, a humanist, a pacifist, an anti-Christian, a vegetarian, or an advocate of a 'one-world' government"—all concepts contrary to their religious beliefs. The Sixth Circuit Court of

Appeals overruled the decision, saying there was no evidence that students, in reading such books, were required to affirm or deny a religious belief or to do anything against their religion. Had the parents been able to prove such coercion, the outcome would undoubtedly have been different. (*Mozert v. Hawkins County Public Schools*, 647 F. Supp. [1986], 827 F. 2d 1058 [1987].)

The second textbook challenge took place in Mobile, Alabama, where a federal judge was presented with the challenge that secular humanism was being promoted in Alabama schools. He agreed with the plaintiffs that this is a form of religion "for First Amendment purposes" because it had been designated as such by the Supreme Court. (The Court did this almost parenthetically in a footnote to a 1961 free exercise opinion that broadened the meaning of the term "religion." *Torasco v. Watkins*, 367 U.S. 488, 495 [1961].) He also agreed that this "religion" was being established by thirty-nine textbooks in history and social studies, all of which unconstitutionally ignored the role of Christianity and Judaism in America and so had to be removed from Alabama's public schools. As expected, the decision was reversed by the Eleventh Circuit Court of Appeals, which saw immediately that designating secular humanism as a religion was simply a springboard for the fundamentalists' legal challenge. But did the texts in question actually promote the beliefs the challengers said they promoted? The appeals court said simply that the purpose behind the thirty-nine texts was clearly not religious, a judgment which surprised no one, since publishers are well aware that promoting an ideology does not sell books. The court indicated, moreover, that the First Amendment requirement that government be neutral toward religion could not be turned "into an affirmative obligation to speak about religion." (*Smith v. Board of School Commissioners,* 665 F. Supp. 939, 827 F. 2d 684 [1987].)

In each of these two cases the law was being used as a last resort to remedy what for the plaintiffs was an intolerable situation, one in which public school texts no longer spoke of their religion or their moral values. A third test of this legal remedy, one that finally reached the Supreme Court in 1987, was the "creation science" controversy. This arose in an effort to protect the literal accuracy of the creation story in Genesis, long felt to be one of the true "fundamentals." This literal accuracy means that Genesis tells us not only who made the universe but precisely how it was made. The discovery of evolution and its eventual appearance in science courses in public schools thus posed an immense threat, because it amassed scientific evidence for a very different "how." For the fundamentalists, evolutionary theory also implied, though scientifically it could never actually say, that there had been no initial creation at all.

Early in this century, laws were passed in many states prohibiting the teaching of evolution outright. All of these were eventually struck down by the Supreme Court. (See *Epperson v. Arkansas,* 393 U.S. 97 [1968].) The fundamentalists then shifted to an equal-time strategy. But for this to work, the Genesis story had to appear to be taught not as a religious alternative to evolution but as a scientific alternative. While most of the scientific evidence advanced by fundamentalists consisted of data attacking evolutionary data, they also constructed tortuous arguments aimed at compressing all events of the earth's history into the few thousand years of biblical chronology and at showing that all fossils are products of a great flood. Because science teachers as a group generally refused to teach these materials as part of their courses, equal time for creation science had to be secured through state laws, two of which were eventually passed in 1981 in Arkansas and Louisiana. (See Dorothy Nelkin, *The Creation Controversy*, Beacon Press, 1982.)

Before dealing with these two state laws, we should note that opposition to biological science does not mean that all fundamentalists are necessarily anti-intellectual. George Marsden insists that learning for them reflects a genuine intellectual tradition going back to the Puritans, but one that is alien to most modern academics. Because they believe that the cultural assumptions of modern thought have undermined the certainties of knowledge, they are much more attracted to the pre-Darwinian philosophical assumption that an objective look at "facts" will bring a higher yield of truth.

It is no accident, for example, that many leaders of the creation science movement have degrees in applied science and engineering and so tend to view the Bible as a collection of true and precise propositions. Henry Morris, the principal architect of creation science theory, has a Ph.D. in hydraulics. He began, he says, with the statements of Genesis and then, "being an engineer, I looked for solid evidence." (Nelkin, *op. cit.*, p. 85.) This compatibility of fundamentalist thought with the technological strand of modern culture explains much of fundamentalism's appeal today. A 1983 Gallup poll came as a great surprise to many because it found that 44 percent of Americans agreed that "God created man pretty much in his present form at one time within the last 10,000 years." (As reported in *The Chronicle of Higher Education*, Dec. 10, 1986.)

But to return to the Arkansas and Louisiana cases, both states passed laws requiring that public school teachers give "balanced treatment" to creation science and evolution; if one was taught, the other also had to be taught. In 1982 a federal judge in Little Rock found that the purpose of creation science was clearly religious and that the Arkansas law violated the establishment clause because the motivation of the legislators was to promote a religious belief. Arkansas did not appeal this decision, but Louisiana did eventually appeal to the Supreme Court when its Creation Act was declared unconstitutional for the same reasons.

Writing in 1987 for a 7-2 majority, Justice Brennan concluded that "the pre-eminent purpose of the Louisiana Legislature was clearly to advance the religious viewpoint that a supernatural being created humankind." He dismissed as a "sham" the legislature's contention that its aim was to foster academic freedom for competing scientific theories on human origins. The Act, he said, "actually serves to diminish academic freedom by removing the flexibility to teach evolution without also teaching creation science." A long dissent by Justice Scalia, joined by Chief Justice

Rehnquist, focused on the "scientific data supporting the theory that the physical universe and life within it appeared suddenly," which they believed was the basis for saying that the legislators had a secular purpose. The law should therefore be upheld, they said, unless further proceedings in a lower court found it unconstitutional on other grounds. (*Edwards v. Aguillard*, 107 S. Ct. 2573, 2581, 2579, 2592 [1987].)

These legal challenges of the fundamentalists serve to throw into sharp relief the contemporary crisis between religious belief systems in America and the widespread indifference to them. Seeking to neutralize Darwinism by requiring public schools to teach fundamentalist doctrine disguised as science may well appear to be a misguided, benighted maneuver, legally doomed from the start. It is nonetheless symptomatic of the larger problem: Moral pluralism threatens the cherished values of large numbers of religious Americans, who now experience the social and religious orders as deeply fragmented. Their strongly held views of society, though perhaps not as extreme as those of the fundamentalists, are not going to go away because of any Supreme Court ruling.

III

Our case study of current discontent among fundamentalist Christians regarding public schools serves to highlight an important fact: The secular undertakings of most Americans may continue to have strong religious underpinnings, but our institutions, our whole mechanisms of government and law, while in many cases they may formally acknowledge the existence and sovereignty of God, cannot of themselves be anything but secular, with essentially secular purposes, namely the maintenance of public order, justice, peace, and freedom. There is nothing specifically religious, much less Christian, about any of these purposes, carried out as they are today in a nation both religously and morally pluralist. This pluralism necessarily entails a continuous struggling together of religious and secular groups, a continuous interplay of opinion that serves, more often than not, to moderate resulting tensions and to urge reconsideration and compromise.

I believe that certain religious groups must have a willingness in the future to accommodate and compromise on the issue of a religious presence in public schools. Their mistake here has not been their concern for this religious presence but their insistence that these schools do what the rest of society has chosen not to do, namely promote common convictions about religious truth and common agreements about moral action. The symbols of this insistence have been prayer and Bible reading in the classroom, and it is now time for many religious people to recognize that compromises have to be made in both these areas. In regard to prayer, for example, it is at present the law of the land that "in this country it is not part of the business of government to compose official prayers for any group of the American people to recite as a part of a religious program carried on by government." (*Engel v. Vitale*, 370 U.S. 421, 425 [1962].) Justice Black was clearly correct in this 1962 opinion: Government, in the guise of public school officials, simply has no competence in this area, however general or inoffensive the wording of any particular classroom prayer may be.

This does not mean that it is not possible to have prayer in public schools. Outside the classroom any official student group may use school facilities to conduct worship services. (*Widmar v. Vincent*, 454 U.S. 263 [1981].) Inside the classroom it is possible for state or local governments to enact "minute of silence" statutes. The Supreme Court has indicated that offering students such opportunities for voluntary silent prayer would not violate the establishment clause. "The legislative intent to return prayer to public schools," said Justice Stevens in 1985, "is, of course, quite different from merely protecting every student's right to engage in voluntary prayer during an appropriate moment of silence during the school day." (*Wallace v. Jaffree*, 472 U.S. 38, 59 [1985].) Hence religious freedom can still be sufficiently accommodated without the enactment of state laws explicitly promoting prayer in the classroom.

Where reconsideration and compromise are most needed, however, is in dealing with religion as an appropriate subject of secular education. Religious people have simply not thought enough about the ways in which public schools can contribute to religious literacy without in the process becoming sectarian. The key question is how precisely to go about studying religious belief, as well as a sacred text such as the Bible. The Supreme Court has stated explicitly that such study itself is appropriate to public education at all levels. It has limited only the devotional use of the Bible, not its pedagogical use. "Nothing we have said here," insisted Justice Clark in the 1963 *Schempp* case, "indicates that . . . study of the Bible or of religion, when presented objectively as part of a secular program of education, may not be effected consistently with the First Amendment." Indeed, he added, "it might well be said that one's education is not complete without a study of comparative religion or of the history of religion and its relationship to the advancement of civilization." (*Abington School District v. Schempp*, 374 U.S. at 225.)

Justice Powell made the same point at greater length in 1987 in his concurring opinion in the creation science case. "As a matter of history," he said,

> "school children can and should properly be informed of all aspects of this Nation's religious heritage. I would see no constitutional problem if school children were taught the nature of the Founding Fathers' religious beliefs and how these beliefs affected the attitude of the time and the structure of our government. . . . In fact, since religion permeates our history, a familiarity with the nature of religious beliefs is necessary to understand many historical as well as contemporary events. . . . The Establishment Clause is properly understood to prohibit the use of the Bible only when the purpose of the use is to advance a particular religious belief." (*Edwards v. Aguillard*, 107 S. Ct. at 2589 – 2590.)

This distinction between teaching the truth of a particular religious belief and teaching about it is crucial. It provides the legal key whereby the Judaeo-Christian tradition, and any other religious tradition, can enter into public school curricula. In the one case religion tends to be divisive, in the other case it is truly educative. Ironically, the chief difficulty in securing this second objective is the paucity of texts on secular subjects that deal adequately with religious themes. An important report issued in 1987 by the Association for Supervision and Curriculum Development suggested guidelines for including matters of religion in the curriculum. It stated flatly:

> "Given the significance of religion and religious movements in the political and cultural history of the world, their virtual absence from today's social studies and history textbooks is particularly reprehensible. . . . Apparently, some people equate any treatment of religion in history texts with advocacy of specific religious ideas and publishers therefore avoid it. . . . Only when educators and parents demand critical instruction about the role of religion in world culture will such passages reappear in reading, literature, science, social studies, and history books." ("Religion in the Curriculum," 55 *Journal of the American Academy of Religion,* 1987, pp. 569 – 588.)

The report goes on to say that many of the assumptions that undergird present policies on religion in the curriculum are "incorrect, contradictory, or illogical." It notes with regret that students today would never know from their textbooks that religious groups were a vital force in the abolitionist and temperance movements of the nineteenth century or in the civil rights movement of the twentieth or that world history and culture were critically influenced by religious thought. It nevertheless recognizes that separating the teaching *of* beliefs from teaching *about* beliefs often means walking a razor's edge. The dilemma will therefore continue to be how to keep both text and teacher neutral on the actual content of belief. That content, while properly the domain of church and home, can nonetheless be the occasion in school for exploration and discussion of moral issues, permitting a student to give expression to ethical insights from his or her own faith.

Those trying to do such teaching "about" religion on the elementary and secondary levels should keep in mind the relatively secure status of religion courses in public-supported colleges. In part this is true because the Supreme Court sees education at this level, as well as the courses themselves, to be voluntary and not mandated by law. College students are also more mature and less susceptible to indoctrination, and the potential of divisiveness is significantly less. (See *Hunt v. McNair*, 413 U.S. 734 [1973].) But this simply means that courses in religion at lower levels need to be very carefully structured. Teachers may be legally prohibited from arguing the case for Judaeo-Christian belief and morality, but it does not follow that concern for children's knowledge of America's religious tradition need be doomed to legal frustration.

What does have to be compromised in this development, then, is any attempt to indoctrinate. Educators and parents may well aspire to create in our elementary and secondary schools some intellectual integration between our predominantly secular public sphere and those religious values still prized by the majority of our citizens. These citizens, in other words, ought not expect to find public school curricula indifferent to religion. But in our present pluralist and progressively more secular society, public schools must inevitably perform a more limited function than they did in the past with respect to inculcating ultimate values. Better and less controversial forums exist to accomplish this laudable goal, namely the family, neighborhood organizations, and church and synagogue. In these forums, moreover, there would be no coercion but rather a manifestation of that voluntary tradition of persuasion which is at the heart of the First Amendment.

IV

The type of accommodation and compromise we have been considering from the point of view of certain religious groups is desirable also on the part of the Supreme Court. This is not only possible but very probable, since there already exists in the Court's establishment jurisprudence a concept known in legal circles as accommodation. The Court has used the concept often but has never defined it. Chief Justice Burger said that it resulted from "play in the joints" between the two religion clauses. Legal scholars now talk about it as a "zone" between the clauses and are beginning to ask how wide this zone should be. (See Michael W. McConnell, "Accommodation of Religion," 1985 *Supreme Court Review*, pp. 1 – 59.) Eventually the Supreme Court will have to answer this question, and perhaps in so doing it will be forced to reconsider some of its past decisions.

The existence of a zone of accommodation was recognized as early as 1952, when Justice Douglas said in the *Zorach* case that when government "encourages religious instruction or cooperates with religious authorities . . . it follows the best of our traditions. For it then respects the religious nature of our people and accommodates the public service to their spiritual needs." (*Zorach v. Clauson*, 343 U.S. 306, 313 [1952].) Douglas was explaining why releasing children for religious instruction away from public school property fell within an area of permissible accommodation, where government regulations may be adjusted to the religious needs of citizens. Otherwise, he said, government would be placed in a position not of neutrality toward religion but of hostility, something clearly at odds with the intention of the Founders. Such allowable government deference we might also call voluntary or discretionary accommodation, to distinguish it from an accommodation so obviously necessary that it would be mandated by the free exercise clause. This voluntary character of the accommodation in question here is precisely what distinguishes it from sponsorship, since the latter by its nature always involves some element of government coercion. In the *Zorach* case there was neither coercion nor sponsorship because public school grounds were not used for religious instruction, nor were students in any way required to attend such instruction.

This distinction between promotion and accommodation lay more or less dormant for almost twenty years after *Zorach,* during which time the Court elaborated what has come to be called the *Lemon* test: For a government practice to be found neutral (and so constitutionally permissible), it must be clear that neither its purpose nor its primary effect is to promote religion, nor must it involve excessive government entanglement with religious bodies. (*Lemon v. Kurtzman,* 402 U.S. 602 [1971].) This three-pronged *Lemon* test has proved to be useful to the Court up to a point, but of itself it begs the question of whether what is at stake in a given case is indeed promotion or only an accommodation. Without this distinction, virtually any government action that seeks to recognize the fact that "we are a religious people" (as Douglas said in *Zorach)* could in principle be construed as having a purpose and effect that violates the establishment clause, thereby placing religion at a permanent disadvantage in society, something clearly not envisioned by the Founders. This did not in fact happen, because the concept of accommodation began to appear once again in Court decisions beginning in 1970.

Conflicts between the two clauses came to a head in 1970 in the landmark *Walz* case, in which the accommodation doctrine received its first extended articulation. The Court was asked whether the traditional property tax exemption for churches was not a promotion and establishment of religion. No, said Chief Justice Burger, the purpose of tax exemption was "not sponsorship since the government does not transfer part of its revenue to churches." It was an effort to "accommodate" religion, by including churches "within a broad class of property owned by non-profit, quasi-public corporations." Such accommodation was a kind of "benevolent neutrality," allowing for "room for play in the joints," neither interfering with religion in a way forbidden by the free exercise clause nor sponsoring it in violation of the establishment clause. (*Walz v. Tax Commission*, 397 U.S. 664, 673, 675 [1970].) To emphasize this last point, Burger pointedly stated that, unlike the mandatory compliance imposed by courts when government is found to violate religious freedom, the voluntary compliance involved in permissible accommodation could not be reduced to a defense of free exercise. It rather existed in a zone between the two clauses, acting in this middle ground as a buffer against conflicts and as a force for harmony.

How wide should this zone of accommodation be? I want to suggest that it ought to be as wide as possible and that, for this to happen, reconsideration and compromise will have to characterize the Court's future approach to disestablishment. While there is obvious need to keep religion and government legally separate, no "perfect absolute separation is really possible," because "we can only dimly perceive the lines of demarcation in this extraordinarily sensitive area of constitutional law." Chief Justice Burger made these statements in 1970 and 1971 (in *Walz, id.* at 670, and in *Lemon*, 402 U.S. at 612) and echoed them in his 1983 ruling in favor of paid legislative chaplains: "The opening of sessions of legislative and other deliberative public bodies with prayer . . . has become part of the fabric of our society" and is "simply a tolerable acknowledgement of beliefs widely held among the people of this country." (*Marsh v. Chambers*, 463 U.S. 783, 786, 792 [1983].)

In 1984, fourteen years after *Walz*, Burger once again spoke for the majority of the Court: "Nor does the Constitution require complete separation of church and state; it affirmatively mandates accommodation, not merely tolerance, of all religions." However, "no fixed *per se* rule can be found," added Burger. While the Court has often found the *Lemon* test helpful, "we have repeatedly emphasized our unwillingness to be confined to any single test or criterion in this sensitive area." (*Lynch v. Donnelly*, 465 U.S. 668, 673, 678, 679 [1984].) In recent years the Court has in fact frequently supplemented the *Lemon* test with the accommodation approach in order to resolve conflicts by seeking a middle ground between the demands of the two clauses.

In 1981, for example, when the University of Missouri at Kansas City refused to allow religious groups to use space for worship, the case was brought to the Court under the establishment clause. But Justice Powell, writing for a majority of eight, focused on the free exercise and equal access rights of the religious groups. Having created a forum open to religious groups, he said, the University could not use a content-based exclusion of religious speech. From the establishment side, he added, such an open forum situation does not of itself confer any state approval of religious practices. (*Widmar v. Vincent*, 454 U.S. at 263.) Two years later, in 1983, a Court majority held constitutional a twenty-eight-year-old Minnesota statute that allows taxpayers to deduct from their state income tax the expense of tuition, textbooks, and transportation of dependents, whether these attend public or private schools. Justice Rehnquist said this did not constitute a support of religion (even though 90 percent of the taxpayers involved sent their children to religious schools) because it "neutrally provides state assistance to a broad spectrum of citizens." He then concluded:

> "The Establishment Clause of course extends beyond prohibition of a state church or payment of state funds to one or more churches. We do not think, however, that its prohibition extends to . . . the sort of attenuated financial benefit, ultimately controlled by the private choices of individual parents, that eventually flows to parochial schools from the neutrally available tax benefit at issue in this case." (*Mueller v. Allen,* 463 U.S. 388, 399, 400 [1983].)

When the type of voluntary accommodation allowed here to Minnesota is denied, however, because the Court applies the *Lemon* test too rigidly, there can be some odd results. This happened in 1985 when a 5-4 majority said that instruction by full-time public school teachers of secular subjects on parochial school premises was unconstitutional. The source of the problem was Title I of the Elementary and Secondary Education Act of 1965, which provides for remedial instruction of impoverished children. In New York City about 200,000 poor children, 22,000 of whom were in parochial schools, were involved in this program. The city had originally required the parochial pupils to travel to public school buildings, but experience showed that to be too difficult. The

city, therefore, decided to do what almost all Title I
programs nationwide were doing, namely to send
teachers into parochial schools during regular class
hours. Supervisors periodically spot-checked to make
certain that instructors stayed clear of religious issues,
thereby ensuring that the clearly secular purpose of
the program did not involve any effect that might
seem to be promoting religion.

Justice Brennan, who wrote for the majority,
acknowledged that this arrangement satisfied the first
two *Lemon* tests, but he said that the supervision that
was involved constituted "excessive entanglement" of
government and so violated the third *Lemon* test.
Justice Rehnquist called this approach a "Catch-22":
Aid must be supervised to ensure that there is no
entanglement, but supervision itself is held to cause
such entanglement. The result was that, after twenty
years without the slightest civic unrest, the line of
separation now had to be drawn at the parochial
school door. Officials around the country are
permitted to teach impoverished children in mobile
trailers on the sidewalk outside or on closed circuit
televison inside or in nearby parks or libraries (all of
which some cities are actually doing), but they
themselves cannot enter the building. This bizarre
situation is based, as Justice O'Connor noted in her
dissent, "on the untenable theory that public school
teachers are likely to start teaching religion merely
because they have walked across the threshold of a
parochial school." *Aguilar v. Felton*, 473 U.S. 402,
413, 420, 431 [1985].)

How far will the Court be willing to go in the future
to accommodate religious conscience? Much will

depend on how rigidly the three-pronged *Lemon* test is understood and applied. The question will always be one of approximation and degree. To what extent is an exclusively religious purpose clearly evident in a given legislative act? How does one measure precisely whether and to what extent some effect promotes religion? At what point does a particular entanglement of religion with government become so significant as to make it unconstitutional? Also, once it is clear that accommodation, not crass sponsorship, is at issue, how meaningful is it to ask whether the accommodation in question has a secular purpose or whether its effect is to encourage or advance religion? Do not all accommodations, including those mandated by the free exercise clause, do this to some extent?

Chief Justice Burger acknowledged in 1971 that

"there are always risks in treating criteria discussed by the Court from time to time as 'tests' in any limiting sense of that term. Constitutional adjudication does not lend itself to the absolutes of the physical sciences or mathematics. The standard should, rather, be viewed as guidelines with which to identify instances in which the objectives of the Religion Clauses have been impaired."

Burger ends (and so can we) by noting again in 1971 that "candor compels the acknowledgment that we can only dimly perceive the boundaries of permissible government activity in this sensitive area of constitutional adjudication." (*Tilton v. Richardson*, 403 U.S. 672, 678 [1971].)

RELIGION AS A
POLITICAL INTEREST GROUP

by

Anthony Champagne

Anthony Champagne

Anthony Champagne was born in Alexandria, Louisiana in 1949. He received his B.A. degree from Millsaps College in 1969 and his M.A. (1971) and Ph.D. (1973) degrees in political science from the University of Illinois. While at the University of Illinois, he was a National Science Foundation trainee and he was a fellow of the Institute for the Study of Law and Behavioral Science at the University of Wisconsin.

Dr. Champagne was an assistant professor and an associate professor at Rutgers University from 1973-1979. In 1979, he came to the University of Texas at Dallas where he is currently a professor in the School of Social Sciences.

He has published two books, one of which was Congressman Sam Rayburn, *acclaimed by both scholarly reviewers and the media. Currently, he is working on a third book on the Texas judiciary which will be titled* Money, Politics, and the Texas Judiciary. *He has edited five other books and has authored or co-authored over thirty scholarly articles as well as several newspaper and magazine pieces.*

Most of his research has dealt with topics related to leadership in the U.S. Congress. Texas politics, the judicial process, and public law, especially constitutional law. His teaching has also been in these areas.

Finally, Dr. Champagne has been the recipient of the AMOCO teaching award twice. He was once a nominee for the Minnie Piper Outstanding Teacher Award. Additionally, he was the first Polykarp Kusch Lecturer at UTD (1985).

RELIGION AS A POLITICAL
INTEREST GROUP

by

Anthony Champagne

Introduction

The thesis of this lecture can be stated very simply: To the extent that the famed "wall of separation" between church and state exists in the United States, it is the Maginot Line of American constitutional law. That is, religion is so deeply engrained in American culture that separation of sectarian and secular concerns is impossible.

For the constitutional scholar or the political theorist, such an argument likely represents a radical departure from the texts of many of the Constitution's framers as well as those who influenced them. It is certainly a departure from the rhetoric found in Supreme Court decisions, particularly since Justice Black's classic exercise of constitutional sleight of hand in *Everson v. Board of Education.* (67 S. Ct. 504 [1947].)

Yet, for persons trained in political jurisprudence and the jurisprudence of legal realism, it should not be surprising that there is a vast gulf between political-legal theory and the reality of American life. Law is full of myths, and one could develop a lengthy list of those myths. For example, the ideas that law is politically neutral and that judges are unbiased and objective decisionmakers are two myths that enjoyed wide credibility in earlier years. Such myths, like the myth of strict separation of church and state, perform valuable political functions. Belief in all three myths, for example, provides legitimacy to the political system. Such beliefs, by building support for the regime, provide for a smoother and more orderly allocation of values in American society than would otherwise take place. The importance of maintaining the myth of separation may have best been described by Mr. Dooley, the cartoon figure that Mr. Justice Frankfurter called "a great philosopher." Said Mr. Dooley, Finley Peter Dunne's Irish political commentator, "Rellijon is a quare thing. Be itself it's all right. . . . Alone it prepares a man f'r a better life. Combined with polyticks it hurries him to it." (Leonard W. Levy, *The Establishment Clause: Religion and the First Amendment*, MacMillan, 1986, p. ix.) When one has, as in America, a situation where religion and politics are mixed, it is important to foster a belief that they are separate. In that way, attempts to create a mixture between the two are kept under control.

It should be clear from the outset of this lecture that I do not reject the regime-sustaining value of the myth of separation of church and state. Strong acceptance of this myth may even discourage some of the more blatant efforts to entangle the two. No one of substance, for example, argues that there should be an established state church in America, and if one did so, there would be nearly universal condemnation of the proposal on the grounds that it is an obvious violation of the Establishment Clause of the Constitution. However, like football, politics is rarely played at such extremes; rather, it tends to be played on a broad middle ground. It is on that broad middle ground that the value of a strict wall of separation becomes debatable and the wall is often either scaled or eluded. It is on that broad middle ground of American politics that I reject the view that a political and social interest as major as religion in American life can be separated from the state. As I view much of the American political scene, religion is such a major interest that the strict wall of separation, such as was envisioned by Roger Williams, then by Thomas Jefferson, and many years later by Hugo Black and a majority of the Supreme Court, is an impossibility.

At the outset of this discussion, I should also emphasize that my argument is not based on any discussion of the intent of the framers. The standard debate over separation of church and state stresses that intent. The strict separationists, of course, emphasize the strong separationist thinking of Thomas Jefferson for support for their perspective. To the separationists, such as Leonard Levy,

"government and religion in America are mutually independent of each other, much as Jefferson and Madison hoped they would be. Government maintains a benign neutrality toward religion. . . . [H]istory has made the wall of separation real. The wall is not just a metaphor. It has constitutional existence. . . . Despite its detractors and despite its leaks, cracks, and its archways, the wall ranks as one of the mightiest monuments of constitutional government in this nation. Robert Frost notwithstanding, something there is that loves a wall." (*Ibid.*, pp. 184 – 185.)

On the other side are the nonpreferentialists, who include such major figures on the political scene as former Secretary of Education William Bennett, former Attorney General Edwin Meese, and Chief Justice William Rehnquist. Their position is that the Establishment Clause forbade a national religion or preference among religious groupings. The primary support for their argument is the long-standing practice of providing tax money on a nonpreferential basis for organized religions. It was a practice that existed in many states long after the adoption of the First Amendment. Essentially, they argue that if the Establishment Clause had called for strict separation, such nonpreferential aid to religion would not have been a common practice in the post-Establishment Clause period in American history. About all that is made clear from attempting to discern whether the framers were separationists or nonpreferentialists is that research on their intent rivals that which passes in these days for Biblical interpretation. I suspect that there is a strong likelihood that it is not possible to resolve the debate over the meaning of the Establishment Clause by focusing on the "muddy brevity" of constitutional text or by examining the very incomplete and often inaccurate records of the Framers. (*Ibid.*, pp. xiv, 187 – 189.)

Even if the intent of the framers is discernible— and substantial evidence can be mustered that the historical evidence will remain unclear enough to make the separationist-nonpreferentialist debate an enduring one—the intent of the framers is largely irrelevant. Religion is and has been such a powerful political interest in America that it cannot be and has not been removed from the political process. Separationists such as Levy may claim that the Establishment Clause functions to depoliticize religion,

> "[separating] government and religion so that we can maintain civility between believers and unbelievers as well as among the several hundred denominations, sects, and cults that thrive in our nation, all sharing the commitment to liberty and equality that cements us together." (*Ibid.*, p. ix.)

However, I believe that the reality of American politics is vastly different from this inspiring mythmaking of Levy's. Religion is a powerful force in the lives of the American people, far more powerful a force than political scientists have traditionally been willing to grant. Religious concerns include a vast number of political, social, and economic issues, ranging from compulsory vaccination laws to sex education to nuclear proliferation. Today, that which is the domain of the state and that which is within the domain of religious faith substantially overlap.

In America, separationists have argued that the overlap between government and religion should be erased. They contend that the Establishment Clause exists to prevent religion—this major political, social, and economic interest—from corrupting the political process. To believe, however, that such a powerful in-

terest can be removed from the political process puts
me in mind of Canute's effort to halt the tide by order-
ing it to stop. As Jack Peltason, an early writer in
political jurisprudence, once wrote, "Litigation, like
legislation, is a stage in the accommodation of interests." (Jack   Peltason,   "The   Interest   Group
Approach," in Glendon Schubert, ed., *Judicial Behavior: A Reader in Theory and Research*, Rand
McNally, 1964, p. 50.) Law, in other words, is a part
of the political process, and law will be an instrument
of interests competing for control over policy. Given
the importance of religion and the strong political interests of religious groups, we should expect law and
government often to accommodate religious interests
rather than to exclude them.

To make this argument, I will first discuss the
pervasiveness of the myth of a strict wall of separation
of church and state. That discussion will be followed
by an examination of the importance of religion in
American life and the key role played by religion in
American politics.

The Myth of the Wall of Separation

In seventeenth-century America, no thinker was a
stronger advocate of the wall of separation than Roger
Williams. Taking for granted that there were natural
law and natural rights, Williams believed that
religious liberty was the most important natural right.
In the 1650s, he wrote strong arguments in favor of
religious liberty and separation of church and state.
Those arguments were actually attacks on the
theocratic government of Massachusetts Bay Colony.

The Bible, Williams argued, made it clear that the state had no responsibility for the soul. Instead, he maintained, compulsory worship "stinks in God's nostrils," denies the Second Coming, and threatens civil peace.

Williams, however, was a radical for his times and was denounced by many in New England as a person of dangerous views. (Alfred H. Kelly and Winfred A. Harbison, *The American Constitution: Its Origins and Development*, W. W. Norton, 1963, pp. 41 – 42.) Even at the time of the framing of the Constitution, his views had not gained widespread acceptance. It should be remembered that other founders of American colonies, such as William Penn, held views that were dramatically different from those of Williams. Penn, for example, wrote, "If we are not governed by God, then we will be ruled by tyrants." (Gary Leeds, "Taking the Bible Seriously," 1987 American Bar Foundation Research Journal 311, 320.) Rhode Island, founded by Williams, and Virginia, heavily influenced by the religious egalitarianism of Thomas Jefferson, James Madison, and James Mason, were the only strong bastions of religious freedom and disestablishment. Officeholders in Delaware and Maryland had to be Christians. In Delaware, they also had to assent to belief in the Trinity and to divine inspiration of the Bible. North Carolina, Pennsylvania, and South Carolina also required officeholders to assent to Biblical divine inspiration, and in Pennsylvania and South Carolina, an officeholder had to assent to a belief in heaven and hell. Maryland, New York, and South Carolina excluded any minister from holding office. Connecticut, Maryland, Massachusetts, New Hampshire, and South Carolina required that only Protestants hold offices, and there were Protestant religious establishments in Connecticut, Georgia, New Hampshire, New Jersey, North Carolina, and South Carolina. It was not until 1833 that the existence of state churches ended in the United States when Massachusetts disestablished the Congregational Church. In the early years of the nineteenth century, New York even required naturalized citizens to deny allegiance to all foreign ecclesiastical figures. (Henry Abraham, *Freedom and the Court: Civil Rights and Liberties in the United States*, Oxford University Press, 1977, p. 249.)

In spite of a substantial entanglement of church and state at the time of the framing of the Constitution, much of the establishment that existed in 1791 was nonpreferential assistance to organized Protestant or Christian religions. A strong argument can be made that it was this type of multiple establishment that the framers attempted to prohibit. In 1784, a bill that provided for tax support of religion had been presented to the Virginia legislature, and Madison attacked it in his "Memorial and Remonstrance against Religious Assessments" so powerfully and so successfully that it was not even presented in the next session of the Virginia legislature. In his remonstrance, Madison made an eloquent argument for separation of church and state:

"What influence in fact have ecclesiastical establishments had on civil society? In some instances they have been seen to erect a spiritual

tyranny on the ruins of civil authority; in many instances they have been seen upholding the
thrones of political tyranny; in no instance have
they been seen the guardians of the liberties of the
people. Rulers who wish to subvert the public
liberty may have found an established clergy con-
venient auxiliaries. A just government, instituted
to secure and perpetuate it, needs them not. Such
a government will be best supported by protecting
every citizen in the enjoyment of his religion with
the same equal hand which protects his person
and his property; by neither invading the equal
rights of any sect, nor suffering any sect to invade
those of another."

As a result of both the debate over the tax and the
effectiveness of Madison's "Remonstrance," Thomas
Jefferson's proposed Statute of Religious Freedom
was passed in 1786. It made religious tests illegal and
allowed for religious freedom. So proud of this document was Jefferson that he instructed that his epitaph
contain mention of the Statute: "On the faces of the
obelisk the following inscription, and not a word
more, 'Here was buried Thomas Jefferson, author of
the Declaration of American Independence, of the
statute of Virginia for religious freedom, and father of
the University of Virginia.'"

Given the importance Jefferson placed on his views
about religious freedom, he would no doubt be
pleased to learn that his thinking is probably the most
frequently cited in the discussions over the need for
separation of church and state. Interestingly, how-

ever, not all of the framers accepted Jefferson's ideas or his leadership. Federalists saw Jefferson as a radical who would import the excesses of the French Revolution. He was, claimed Chief Justice Oliver Ellsworth, a "visionary." And, it should be noted, Ellsworth did not consider the word to be a compliment. Secretary of State John Marshall, soon to be Chief Justice Marshall, felt that Jefferson as President would "sap the fundamental principles of government." Worse, other Federalists considered Jefferson to be a "howling atheist." (John A. Garraty, "The Case of the Missing Commissions," in John A. Garraty, ed., *Quarrels That Have Shaped the Constitution*, Harper and Row, 1964, p. 1.) Associate Justice Joseph Story felt it important that Jefferson's "fallacies" be refuted. It was a mistake, believed Story, for Jefferson's view that Christianity was not "indispensable to the true interests and solid foundation for all government" to go unanswered. (Leeds, p. 317, n. 25.)

By today's standards, some of the language of both Madison's "Remonstrance" and Jefferson's statute would raise questions of establishment. Madison's "Remonstrance" asked God's help in opposing the tax to support religion:

> "[We oppose] so dangerous an usurpation . . .
> earnestly praying . . . that the Supreme Lawgiver
> of the universe, by illuminating those to whom it
> is addressed, may on the one hand turn their
> councils from every act which would affront His
> holy prerogative, or violate the trust committed to
> them; and on the other, guide them into every
> measure which may be worthy of His blessing,

may redound to their own praise, and establish more firmly the liberties . . . of the Commonwealth."

Jefferson wrote in the Statute of Religious Freedom that "Almighty God has created the mind free" and that attempts to restrict freedom of the mind are "a departure from the plan of the Holy Author. . . ."

Perhaps these small breaches in the wall of separation may be treated as mere religious rhetoric in the battle for religious freedom; Jefferson and Madison did try very hard as Presidents to maintain strict separation of church and state. Both refused to issue Thanksgiving Day proclamations on the grounds that such statements violated the principle of non-establishment, and both considered tax exemptions for churches, government pay for congressional and military chaplains, and nonpreferential land grants for the support of churches to be unconstitutional. Even Jefferson, however, described by Leonard Levy as an even more extreme separationist than Madison, made an Indian treaty which provided federal money for tribal religious needs and missionary expenses to "propagate the Gospel among the Heathen." (Levy, p. 183.) The heyday of the effectiveness of the wall of separation may have been even earlier than the Jefferson and Madison Administrations. The 1796 treaty with Tripoli, which was negotiated during the administration of President Washington and was ratified by the U.S. Senate, stated that there were no grounds for any religious differences between Tripoli and the United States of America because "the government of the United States of America is not, in

any sense, founded on the Christian religion."
(C. Herman Pritchett, *The American Constitution*,
McGraw Hill, 1968, p. 569.)

Strict as were the views of Jefferson, Madison, and
others in the early years of this country, the Supreme
Court was slow to discover the wall of separation. And
its awareness of and reliance upon the wall of separation has had such a variable history that Levy has
claimed, "The Supreme Court has been inexcusably
inconsistent in its interpretation of the establishment
clause." (Levy, p. 162.) There is, however, a strong
thread of strict separationist thinking in Supreme
Court opinions on establishment, thinking which goes
back at least to the late nineteenth century.

In 1878, George Reynolds was indicted for bigamy
in the Territory of Utah. The case ultimately went to
the U.S. Supreme Court on a number of grounds, the
relevant one for our purposes being Reynolds's claim
that his marriages were in furtherance of his sense of
religious duty and that therefore he should not be
held guilty of a crime. Reynolds, a Mormon, argued
that his church taught that it was the duty of its male
members to practice polygamy and that such teaching
was based on the Bible and upon a revelation to
Joseph Smith, the church's founder and prophet.
Failure of a male member of the church to practice
polygamy if he were able to do so would lead to
"damnation in the life to come." (Reynolds v. United
States, 98 U.S. 145, 161 [1879].) In an opinion by
Chief Justice Morrison Waite, the Court traced the
development of the concept of the establishment of
religion, and Waite emphasized how important
Madison and Jefferson viewed a ban on establish-

ment. Waite noted that when Jefferson first saw the initial draft of the Constitution, he expressed disappointment that it lacked a guarantee of freedom of religion. The ban on establishment was proposed by Madison and others during the first Congress. Quickly adopted, that ban was strongly supported by Jefferson, who argued:

> "Believing with you that religion is a matter which lies solely between man and his God; that he owes account to none other for his faith or his worship; that the legislative powers of the government reach actions only, and not opinions,—I contemplate with sovereign reverence that act of the whole American people which declared that their legislature should make 'no law respecting an establishment of religion or prohibiting the free exercise thereof,' thus building a wall of separation between church and state." (*Ibid.*, p. 164.)

All the while insisting that the Court was adhering to Jefferson's views, Waite found that marriage, which this separationist Chief Justice described as "a sacred obligation," was a contract which could be regulated by law (*Reynolds v. United States*, 165.) Indeed, he noted that polygamy had long been banned by Western European states. By the time of James I, Waite added, polygamy was punishable by death. There was historical evidence that the practice was odious to all nations except, noted Waite (in what he must have thought was a wry aside), among "Asiatic and . . . African people." (*Ibid.*, 164.) Additionally, he stated that "polygamy would destroy the social condition" and lead to patriarchy which "fetters the people in stationary despotism." (*Ibid.*, 166.) Thus, while the wall of separation must be maintained, Mr. Reynolds was ordered to serve two years in prison and to pay a $500 fine. Although Waite did stress that laws could punish acts related to religious beliefs, such as punishing the practitioner of polygamy, the practitioner of human sacrifice, or the wife who attempts to jump upon the burning funeral pyre of her dead husband, laws "cannot," wrote Waite, "interfere with mere religious beliefs and opinions." (*Ibid.*, 166.)

Waite's statement giving absolute protection to religious beliefs and opinions must have been welcomed by Samuel Davis, who in 1890 was held to be disqualified as a voter in the Territory of Idaho because, as a Mormon, he believed in polygamy. Although Davis in order to vote had to swear an oath that he "[abjured] bigamy or polygamy" (*Davis v. Beason*, 133 U.S. 333 [1890]), a unanimous Court offered a clever defense of the wall of separation: "[E]very one under the jurisdiction of the United States [may] entertain notions respecting his relations to his Maker and the duties they impose as may be approved by his judgment and conscience, and to exhibit his sentiments in such form of worship as he may think proper. . . ." (*Ibid.*, 341–342.) After reading this separationist language, Davis must have been surprised to learn that, nevertheless, he could not vote because of his belief in polygamy. Justice Field, the opinion's author, argued that such a ban was necessary to ensure that peace and order were maintained. Mr. Davis's belief in polygamy, according to the Court, interfered with the morals of the people. It was not to be the last time that the Court was to give a ringing argument for separation of church and state, only to conclude with a justification for the entanglement of the two.

Perhaps the most famous example of such an approach to separation is *Everson v. Board of Education.* (67 S. Ct. 504 [1947].) *Everson* dealt with the constitutionality of a New Jersey township Board of Education's authorization of bus transportation for parochial school children. In his opinion for a badly split Court, Justice Black wrote that the Establishment Clause meant at least the following:

"Neither a state nor the Federal Government can set up a church. Neither can pass laws which aid one religion, aid all religions, or prefer one religion over another. Neither can force nor influence a person to go to or to remain away from church against his will or force him to profess a belief or disbelief in any religion. No person can be punished for entertaining or professing religious beliefs or disbeliefs, for church attendance or nonattendance. No tax in any amount, large or small, can be levied to support any religious activities or institutions, whatever they may be called, or whatever form they may adopt to teach or practice religion. Neither a state nor the Federal Government can, openly or secretly, participate in the affairs of any religious organizations or groups and vice versa. In the words of Jefferson, the clause against establishment of religion by law was intended to erect 'a wall of separation between Church and State.'" (*Ibid.*, 511–512.)

Later in the opinion, Justice Black wrote, "The First Amendment has erected a wall between church and state. That wall must be kept high and impregnable. We could not approve the slightest breach." (*Ibid.*, 513.) Justice Black, of course, is well known as the author of unusually powerful Court opinions, and *Everson* is one where even the great Hugo Black outdid himself; however, as Justice Robert Jackson wrote in dissent in *Everson*, it is an opinion which puts him in mind of Byron's report of his seduction of Julia, who, claimed Byron, "whispering 'I will ne'er consent,'—consented." (*Ibid.*) Black, of course, allowed the Board of Education to continue providing bus transportation reimbursement to parents of parochial school children. There was, claimed Black, no penetration of the wall of separation since the beneficiary of the aid was not religion but the children who were aided in being transported "regardless of religion, safely and expeditiously to and from accredited schools. . . ." (*Ibid.*)

In 1963, the Court was again faced with an establishment issue, this one pointing to the dilemma that can be created by an insistence on strict separation of church and state. In *Sherbert v. Verner* (374 U.S. 398 [1963]), a Seventh-Day Adventist was denied unemployment compensation because she was unwilling to accept available work on Saturday. While applicants for unemployment compensation were not required to accept available employment on Sunday, there were no allowances for those whose religious day was Saturday. It was acknowledged that the law was not designed to discriminate against Seventh-Day Adventists; rather the burden on Seventh-Day Adventists was an indirect effect of the law's effort to encourage participation in the work force. Nevertheless, the Court required that an exception be created such that Seventh-Day Adventists be allowed to refuse available Saturday employment and remain eligible for unemployment compensation. The Court was trying to prevent the state through its unemployment compensation regulations from interfering unduly with the free exercise of religion that is guaranteed by the Constitution. However, as Justice Harlan pointed out in dissent, to carve out an exception to a law for religious reasons seems to go far beyond the principle of neutrality of the state in religious matters that was suggested by the majority. As Harlan saw the decision, it meant that states "must single out for financial assistance those whose behavior is religiously motivated, even though it denied such assistance to others whose identical behavior . . . is not religiously motivated." (*Ibid.*, 422). While Harlan did not go so far as to insist that allowing for free exercise can create a violation of the Establishment Clause, that point is at least implied by his reasoning. (See also Philip B. Kurland, *Religion and the Law*, Aldine Publishing, 1962.) One can therefore expand upon Harlan's thinking and suggest that a definition of non-establishment as strict separation of church and state can directly conflict with a state's effort to accommodate religious exercise.

In 1984, the Supreme Court in *Lynch v. Donnelly* (465 U.S. 668 [1984]) was faced with a major case dealing with the wall of separation between church and state. Pawtucket, Rhode Island, erected a Christmas display. That display not only included such figures as Santa, his reindeer, a clown, candy canes, and carolers, it also include a creche consisting of the Infant Jesus, Mary, Joseph, angels, shepherds, kings, and animals. The city had purchased the creche for $1365 in 1973, and except for lighting expenses, the creche cost the city only about $20 a year to erect and dismantle. Yet, this display of Christ's birth obviously scales the wall of separation. To his credit, Chief Justice Burger, the author of the Court's opinion, did not play word games and write that he was using a rigid view of the Establishment Clause. Although in *Larkin v. Grendel's Den*, Chief Justice Burger went so far as to praise the concept of the "wall of separation" as a "useful signpost" which was helpful in emphasizing the separateness of church and state (103 S. Ct. 505, 510 [1982]), that wall crumbled in Burger's hands in *Lynch v. Donnelly*. Instead, he argued, one should determine whether an establishment exists by inquiring

> "whether the challenged law or conduct has a secular purpose, whether its principal or primary effect is to advance or inhibit religion, and whether it creates an excessive entanglement of government with religion. But we have repeatedly emphasized our unwillingness to be confined to any single test or criterion in this sensitive area." (*Ibid.*, 678.)

In other words, while there is some degree of separation of church and state, there is no rigid separation. Burger kept the definition of separation deliberately vague. Lacking the rhetorical strength of Hugo Black, he was nevertheless as capable as Black when it came to misleading his readers. Claimed Burger, "[T]he Court consistently has declined to take a rigid, absolutist view of the Establishment Clause." (*Ibid.*, 678.) Unfortunately, he also found it necessary to stress the facts of the case in an effort to show that the wall of separation was not being seriously breached. He noted that the creche was on display with such nonreligious symbols as Santa and reindeer, which showed the nonreligious significance of the display. (See Justice Brennan's forceful dissent, especially at 708; see also Levy, p. 177; contrast with Justice Burger's denial at 685, n. 12.) Ineffectively written and reasoned as *Lynch* may be, at least it is the case, as Andrew Cecil has written, that *Lynch* is a sign

"of a shift in the Supreme Court's position toward official acknowledgement of the role of religion in American life. . . . [A] trend may be discerned toward the accommodation of religion to public life, as long as there is no 'real danger of establishment of a state church.' Such an accommodation recognizes that political issues also have moral and ethical dimensions which have always and will continue to remain a part of the concerns of religion." (Andrew R. Cecil, "The Unchanging Spirit of Freedom," in W. Lawson Taitte, ed., *Traditional Moral Values in the Age of Technology,* The University of Texas at Dallas, 1987, p. 172.)

That shift, I will argue in the following sections, is a recognition of the reality of the strength of religion as a political interest in America.

The Pervasiveness of Religion in America

Those who feel that religion and the revived evangelical movement have been insignificant forces in American political life and debate in the 1970s and 1980s should keep in mind that the number of persons who may in any way be described as political activists is also small. For example, in 1980 only 7 percent of the population had contributed to any political action group, only 8 percent had attended a political meeting or rally, and only 37 percent voted in their state's primary election. On the other hand, 21 percent frequently listened to religious radio, 28 percent frequently read the Bible, 32 percent watched religious television in the week prior to the survey, 62 percent participated in church social activities, and 72 percent had attended church in the previous six months. Four percent of Americans claim to speak in tongues. That is more than the percentage of Americans who worked in behalf of a candidate or a political party in 1980. It is only 1 percent less than the percentage of the population who contributed $1 through their income tax payment to the presidential campaign fund. (Kenneth D. Wald, *Religion and Politics in the United States*, St. Martin's Press, 1987, p. 9.)

The degree of religiosity in America is strong enough that public opinion would reverse the line of the Supreme Court decisions that banned prayer in the public schools. A 1983 Gallup poll found that 82 percent of respondents had heard of the proposed amendment to the U.S. Constitution which would allow voluntary prayer in the public schools. Of those, 81 percent favored the amendment, which would essentially reverse the Supreme Court; 14 percent opposed it; and 5 percent had no opinion. Interestingly, not only did a substantial majority of the respondents favor the amendment to place voluntary prayer back in the public schools, but they had strong feelings about the issue: 48 percent of respondents very strongly favored the amendment; 29 percent fairly strongly favored it; and only 4 percent favored it not at all strongly. Of those opposing the amendment, 2 percent opposed it not at all strongly, 5 percent opposed the amendment fairly strongly, and 7 percent opposed it very strongly. (George H. Gallup, *The Gallup Poll: Public Opinion 1983*, Scholarly Resources, p. 172.)

Walter Burnham noted that, if nothing else, the 1980 presidential election—with the Moral Majority's heavy involvement in the election, with the Catholic Archdiocese of Boston campaigning against proabortion candidates in Massachusetts, with Carter, Reagan, and Anderson all professing to be "born again," and with 40 percent of probable voters claiming to have had a personal experience of Jesus Christ—indicated that America is, statistically at least, God's country. (Walter D. Burnham, "Appendix A, Social Stress and Political Response: Religion and the 1980 Election," in Thomas Ferguson and Joel

Rogers, eds., *The Hidden Election: Politics and Economics in the 1980 Presidential Campaign,* Pantheon Books, 1981, p. 132.)

The great importance of religion to Americans is nicely shown by a plot of a regression equation prepared by Burnham. A measure of national development was regressed and was plotted against responses from a 1976 international Gallup poll in which the respondents were asked whether their religious beliefs were very important, fairly important, not too important, or not at all important. Fourteen countries or regional areas were used in the analysis. With the exception of the United States (and to a lesser extent Canada), there is a clear and very strong relationship between religiosity and development such that the more developed the country, the less important is religion to its citizenry. The United States, the major exception to this pattern, as is noted in Figure 1, is far more religious than would be predicted by its level of development. Of the Americans polled, 56 percent said that their religious beliefs were "very important" to them. That high level of religiosity is about what would be expected from countries with development levels of Chile, Mexico, Lebanon, or Portugal. To put it another way, the United States has a level of development such that the regression equation would predict that approximately 0 percent of Americans, instead of the actual 56 percent figure, would consider their religious beliefs very important. Burnham, clearly impressed by the uniqueness of America in comparison to other countries, stressed that "the extraordinary persistence of religious commitments as such must be regarded as

FIGURE 1
RELIGION AND DEVELOPMENT:
RELATIONSHIP BETWEEN 1976 GALLUP RESPONSES SAYING
THAT RELIGIOUS BELIEFS WERE "VERY IMPORTANT"
TO RESPONDENTS AND COUNTRY SCORES ON
A MEASURE OF NATIONAL DEVELOPMENT

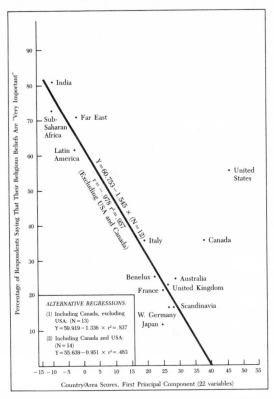

Sources: For the data on religious beliefs: *Gallup Opinion Index* (American Institute of Public Opinion), "Religion in America 1976." For the data on the developmental index: first principal component based on 22 development variables, J. P. Cole, *Geography of World Affairs*, Penguin, 1979. Situation as of 1973. For the regression analysis: Walter Dean Burnham, "Appendix A, Social Stress and Political Response; Religion and the 1980 Election," in Thomas Ferguson and Joel Rogers, eds., *The Hidden Election: Politics and Economics in the 1980 Presidential Campaign*, Pantheon Books, 1981, p. 135.

an autonomous constraint of profound importance." (*Ibid.*, p. 134.) Indeed, he suggested that most Europeans would have nothing in their experience which would allow them to comprehend American religiosity and that the wide gulf between America and the developed world in reference to religion could be an explanation for the "notorious lack of rapport or understanding" between Chancellor Schmidt and President Carter. (*Ibid.*)

Given the importance of religion to Americans, we would also expect religion to loom as a major consideration in domestic politics and to be a major and particularly visible force in presidential politics.

Voting and Presidential Politics

Claims of a belief in the wall of separation were insufficient to be of much help to the 1928 Democratic nominee for the presidency. That presidential candidate, Al Smith, tried unsuccessfully to separate his religion from the secular world of presidential electoral politics. Herbert Hoover defeated him badly, in part because Smith was a Catholic. (Anthony Champagne, *Sam Rayburn: A Biobibliography*, Greenwood Press, 1988, p. 16.) Smith attempted to thwart opposition to his Catholicism by claiming that he was a believer "in the absolute separation of Church and State and in the strict enforcement of the provisions of the Constitution that Congress shall make no law respecting an establishment of religion or prohibiting the free exercise thereof. ("Catholic and Patriot: Governor Smith Replies," in John F. Wilson and Donald L. Drakeman, eds., *Church and*

State in American History, Beacon Press, 1987, p.
186.) Smith's ties to Tammany, his progressive record
as governor, and his antiprohibition stand all greatly
contributed to his defeat at the hands of Herbert
Hoover. (Champagne, p. 16.) Yet the religious bigotry
of the voters was clearly present, and they were not
appeased by Smith's separationist perspective.

Religion can be injected into presidential (and congressional) politics on a scale far smaller than the
grand forum of a presidential election. Of many
possible examples, one that is quite appropriate given
the politics surrounding the Pledge of Allegiance in
the 1988 presidential campaign, deals with the inser-
tion of the words "under God" in the pledge. The
Reverend George M. Docherty, a Scottish émigré,
studied the Pledge of Allegiance and came to the conclusion that

> "that which was missing was the characteristic and
> definitive factor in the American way of life. In-
> deed, apart from the mention of the phrase 'the
> United States of America,' it could be the pledge
> of any republic. In fact, I could hear little Mosco-
> vites [sic] repeat a similar pledge to their hammer-
> and-sickle flag in Moscow with equal solemnity.
> Russia is also a republic that claims to have
> overthrown the tyranny of kingship. Russia also
> claims to be indivisible." (Quoted in Mark Silk,
> *Spiritual Politics: Religion and America Since
> World War II,* Simon and Schuster, 1988, p. 96.)

Reverend Docherty argued that the definitive factor
in American life was God and that the pledge should

be amended to read "one nation *under God*." (*Ibid.*, p. 96.)

The Supreme Board of the Knights of Columbus had made such a proposal three years earlier, and in 1953 Congressman Louis Rabaut had introduced legislation in the House to amend the pledge. When Reverend Docherty delivered his sermon on February 7, 1954, suggesting the amendment to the pledge, one sympathetic member of the congregation was President Dwight D. Eisenhower. Within days, seventeen bills to amend the pledge were introduced in the Congress. Although the Senate Judiciary Committee had qualms over the implications of the amendment for the separation of church and state, pressure built to the point where the Senate eventually unanimously supported the bill. The bill also rapidly moved through the process in the House, aided by an outpouring of favorable constituent mail, radio commentator support, the Hearst press, and a variety of veterans, civic, fraternal, patriotic, labor, and trade groups. While the Association of Unitarian Ministers in Boston protested that the inclusion of God in the pledge was an invasion of religious liberty, its assertions were ignored. (*Ibid.*, pp. 96–98.)

Arrangements were made for the President to sign the bill on June 14, 1954, Flag Day. There would be a flag-raising ceremony at the Capitol which would be the culmination of an American Legion drive to encourage people to fly the flag. When the legislation passed, its House and Senate sponsors recited the amended pledge in unison before Walter Cronkite and the CBS cameras, which broadcast the ceremony under the title "New Glory for Old Glory." (*Ibid.*, p.

98.) At the signing ceremony for the bill, President Eisenhower stated his pleasure over the fact that schoolchildren in America would proclaim "the dedication of our Nation and our people to the Almighty." The amended pledge was a statement of "our country's true meaning." Also, it was a way to strengthen "those spiritual weapons which forever will be our country's most powerful resource, in peace or in war." (*Ibid.*) Congressional leaders were quick to interpret the significance of this ritual wedding of God and flag. Congressman Rabaut, the House sponsor of the amendment, stated, "You and I know that the Union of Soviet Socialist Republics would not, and could not, while supporting the philosophy of communism, place in its patriotic ritual an acknowledgement that their nation existed 'under God.'" (*Ibid.*) Senator Ferguson, the Senate sponsor of the amendment, added that the amended pledge was a way to highlight the differences between freedom and communism. Congressman Overton Brooks of Louisiana, with an eloquence powered by patriotic fervor, stated that the amended pledge was an open declaration "that we denounce the pagan doctrine of communism and declare 'under God' in favor of free government and a free world." (*Ibid.*, pp. 98 – 99.) Shortly thereafter, the Congress saw fit to also declare that all U.S. coins and paper currency would bear the slogan "In God We Trust," and that statement was to become the official U.S. motto in 1956. Congress in 1955 created a nondenominational prayer center in the Capitol. In a show of religious bipartisanship, this scaling of the wall of separation was done with the advice of the two congressional chaplains (both Protestant), the assistant chancellor of the Catholic Archdiocese of Washington, and the rabbi of the Washington Hebrew Congregation. In 1956, Congress declared that all first- and second-class mail would be cancelled with a stamp saying "Pray for Peace." Such a cancellation stamp, it was claimed by the bill's sponsor, would remind us of "our dependence upon God and of our faith in His support." (*Ibid.*, p. 100.) Given this political-religious fervor, it is somewhat surprising that Senator Ralph Flanders was unsuccessful in his proposal to amend the Constitution to recognize the authority and law of Jesus Christ. Even in the Congress's version of the Great Awakening, there were apparently limits on the extent to which the wall of separation would be dismantled. (For a detailed treatment of the politics of the wording in the Pledge of Allegiance, see *ibid.*, pp. 96 – 100.)

It was the allegedly separationist Justice William Brennan who was to offer the rationalization for the constitutionality of such religious practices as those that concerned the Congress in the mid-1950s. Like Black in *Everson*, he insisted upon adhering to the myth of separation while allowing these practices on the grounds that they were devoid of religious meaning. (For an elaboration of these ideas, see Justice Brennan's concurring opinion in *School District of Abington Township v. Schempp*, 374 U.S. 203, especially 296 – 304 [1963].)

Even in 1960, there were many persons who felt that a Catholic President would be governed by the Church hierarchy. When, on September 7, 1960, a group of Protestant ministers and laypersons meeting in Houston, Texas, issued a statement claiming that the Catholic Church would govern Kennedy's political decisions if he were elected President, the candidate realized that he had to resolve such doubts in his favor. On September 12, 1960, Kennedy met with the Greater Houston Ministerial Association and discussed the "religious issue." He said, "I believe in an America where the separation of church and state is absolute." Never mind that absolute separation is impossible, Kennedy went further and claimed that he also believed that it should be the case in America that "no religious body seeks to impose its will directly or indirectly upon the general populace or the public acts of its officials." If that was not enough, he also believed in an America "where there was no Catholic vote, no anti-Catholic vote, no bloc voting of any kind; and where Catholics, Protestants, and Jews, at both the lay and pastoral level, will refrain from those attitudes of disdain and division which have so often marred their works in the past, and promote instead the American ideal of brotherhood."

As is so typical of Kennedy's major speeches, it is an eloquent and moving statement, one which many feel turned the issue of religion in his favor. Sam Rayburn, himself a Primitive Baptist who had campaigned for Al Smith in 1928 and who concluded that a Catholic could not be elected President, was impressed with the speech and with Kennedy's performance. Kennedy so overwhelmed the Houston ministers that, said Rayburn, Kennedy "ate them blood raw." (Champagne, pp. 59 – 60.)

The speech was a statement of separationist philosophy that would have made Roger Williams proud.

However, the reality of the American political system is vastly different from Kennedy's desire for an "absolute separation of church and state." Kennedy gave his acclaimed speech to the Houston ministers on September 12, 1960. Two days later, according to the Robert F. Kennedy Papers at the John F. Kennedy Library, a Harris poll was run in Texas which asked Texans if they were concerned "over having a Catholic in the White House." On October 17, a second poll was conducted in Texas in which the same question was asked. Immediately prior to the election, on November 3, a third poll asked the same question. As Table 1 shows, in the aftermath of Kennedy's famous speech, 37 percent of Texas voters were concerned about having a Catholic in the White House, and in the two subsequent polls that figure increased to 42 percent. Of the voters who said that they were going to vote for Kennedy, 82 percent on September 14 said that they were not concerned about having a Catholic in the White House, 81 percent of those responding to the poll on October 17 said they were not concerned, and 84 percent responding on November 3 said that they were not concerned. However, of those who said that they were voting for Richard Nixon, 58 percent were concerned about a Catholic being in the White House in the first poll, 61 percent were concerned in the second poll, and 66 percent were concerned in the poll conducted immediately before the election. Clearly, roughly four of ten voters in Texas in 1960 had worries about a Catholic President, and Richard Nixon appears to have benefited considerably from those prejudices.

TABLE 1

Concern Over Having a Catholic in the White House

	9-14-60 Poll			10-17-60 Poll			11-3-60 Poll		
	Total Voters	*Voting for Nixon*	*Voting for Kennedy*	*Total Voters*	*Voting for Nixon*	*Voting for Kennedy*	*Total Voters*	*Voting for Nixon*	*Voting for Kennedy*
Concerned	42%[1]	66%	16%	42%	61%	19%	37%	58%	18%
Not Concerned	58%	34%	84%	58%	39%	81%	63%	42%	82%

[1] Absolute numbers and margin of error were not reported. Source: The polls were conducted by Louis Harris. These poll data were found in the John F. Kennedy Library in Robert F. Kennedy's files on polls on the 1960 election.

Separation of church and state and religious tolerance in America certainly did not apply to the presidential electoral process in 1960. Even some Catholics attacked the notion of a Catholic presidential candidate. A group of Catholics took out full-page advertisements in the Houston papers claiming that they were opposed to Kennedy because his campaign has "fostered the religious issue" and because his campaign displayed "two-edged bigotry." (O. Douglas Weeks, *Texas in the 1960 Presidential Election*, Institute of Public Affairs, 1961, p. 59.)

In more recent times, two Presidents, Jimmy Carter and Ronald Reagan, and presidential candidate John Anderson have proclaimed themselves "born again" and have welcomed the votes of those who see no wall between a candidate's religious views and his fitness for the presidency. Reagan, Carter, and Anderson were cultivating the supporters of the revival of traditional religion. William Jennings Bryan had, in the late nineteenth century and the early twentieth century, captured the support of evangelical Protestants; however, with the departure of Bryan the evangelical movement in politics tended to die down, with only minor eruptions such as opposition to John Kennedy's candidacy in 1960, considerable support for Barry Goldwater in 1964 and for George Wallace in 1968, and opposition to the Equal Rights Amendment in the early 1970s. The fact that most of the states that failed to ratify the ERA had either substantial numbers of Mormons (Utah, Nevada, and Arizona) or large numbers of evangelical Protestants (every state of the Old Confederacy except Texas and Tennessee) did not go unnoticed by politicians and by political activists. Additionally, evangelicals became active in opposition to some school textbooks and to gay rights ordinances. They viewed many texts, gay rights, and the ERA as challenges to traditional morality. (Wald, pp. 183 – 193.)

Howard Phillips, Terry Dolan, Paul Weyrich, and Richard Vigurie had previously had no involvement in the evangelical movement, but they lent to evangelical leaders their organizations—the Conservative Caucus, the National Conservative Political Action Committee, and the National Committee for the Survival of a Free Congress—their organizational skills, and their fund-raising talents. They proposed the formation of an evangelical coalition which would attack "big government" and support traditional moral and economic values. The idea was to move evangelicals into supporting a comprehensive conservative social program which would include opposition to gun control, the Panama Canal treaty, abortion, the union shop, and cuts in the defense budget. The results of this alliance between evangelical leaders and conservative political activists were three organizations: the Moral Majority, the Religious Roundtable, and Christian Voice. Positions of these groups were wide-ranging, and at times the leaders of these groups were quite creative in justifying their positions. More money was needed for national defense, for example, on the grounds that a strong defense would keep the country free for preaching God's Word. Similarly, it was necessary to support the governments of Taiwan and South Africa because they were Christian allies in opposition to godless Communism. Reverend Falwell found it necessary to oppose

secular humanism through low inflation politics, flat-
rate taxation, and a balanced federal budget, and he
was able to discern a basis for these policies in the
Scriptures. (*Ibid.*, pp. 188–191.)

Reagan's margins of victory in 1980 and in 1984
were so great that they cannot be ascribed solely to
support by this new evangelical movement. It is unclear how politically influential the movement has
been in national or congressional politics; the Gallup
organization has estimated their numbers at about 20
percent of the voting-age population, although the
methodology for this estimate is questionable since
approximately one in four of Gallup's so-called
evangelicals are black and perhaps 10–15 percent
more of Gallup's evangelicals are Catholics. Nevertheless, evangelicals are widely attributed to have
defeated a Republican Congressman from Alabama in
1980 and to have made Jesse Helms the victor in the
notorious Helms-Hunt Senate race in North Carolina
in 1984. It is also the case, however, that national
polls have shown Reverend Falwell to be one of the
least popular national figures and the Moral Majority
to be one of the least-liked national organizations.
(*Ibid.*, pp. 201–206.) Generally, the American public
is hostile to overt political activity by religious groups.
In 1980, for example, a Gallup poll asked whether
religious groups were right or wrong to work actively
for the defeat of political candidates who disagreed
with their position on certain issues. Only 12 percent
of the respondents said that the religious groups were
right, 60 percent said they were wrong, and 12
percent were undecided. They were also asked
whether it was right or wrong for a Catholic Cardinal

to say it was a sin to vote for political candidates who favored abortion. Only 27 percent said it was right, 59 percent said it was wrong, and 14 percent were undecided. Even among Catholics, only 33 percent said the Cardinal was right to make such a statement. (George Gallup, *The Gallup Poll: Public Opinion 1980*, Scholarly Resources, pp. 238–239.) Yet the evangelical movement has had some successes. The ERA has been defeated, federal funds are no longer used for abortions, and schools must give religious groups "equal access." Other issues remain on the national political agenda as a result of activities by evangelicals. These issues include a reversal of *Roe v. Wade*, an amendment to allow prayer in the public schools, and, in many areas of the country, a moment of silent meditation in the public schools. (Wald, p. 206.)

By the 1980 presidential campaign, these groups had gained considerable media attention and were actively supporting the candidacy of Ronald Reagan. Although both Anderson and Carter would seem to be personally more appealing to evangelicals than Reagan—a Hollywood actor, divorced, and the father of children who did not represent traditional values—Reagan had exerted a strong personal appeal over the movement. Unlike Carter and Anderson, Reagan also endorsed the position of evangelical leaders and expressed support for their political agenda. By 1984, the evangelical movement was reputable enough that Reverend James Robison, a former vice president of the Religious Roundtable, was the minister who opened the Republican Convention with a prayer and Reverend Falwell, the president of the Moral Majority, closed it with the designation of Ronald Reagan and George Bush as "God's instruments in rebuilding America." (*Ibid.*, pp. 193–194.)

Although representatives of the religious right were somewhat discredited in 1988 by scandals in evangelical quarters, the Democratic Party had a progressive Baptist minister make a strong bid for the presidency. Less impressive was the showing in the Republican Party of fundamentalist minister Pat Robertson, although he promised that 1988 would not be his last try for the presidency. The importance of religious symbols was stressed by the visibility given to the Greek Orthodox cleric who sat in the convention VIP booth next to Barbara Bush and who conspicuously applauded Vice President Bush's acceptance speech. Also given significant airtime were two Catholic bishops who declared that they had abandoned the Democratic Party because of its proabortion stand. (James C. Harrington, "Why Must We Argue Over a Loyalty Oath?" Texas Lawyer, October 3, 1988, p. 22.)

How religion plays itself out on the political stage will be explored in the next three sections, which will examine (1) "Religion, Congress, and Congressional Votes"; (2) "Judicial Selection and Judicial Decision-making"; and (3) "Religion as a Political Lobby."

Religion, Congress, and Congressional Votes

The wall of separation is evaded by far more than the evangelical movement. The pervasiveness of religion in the American polity can clearly be seen by recent research on the effect of religion upon Congressmen and their congressional voting behavior. Peter L. Benson and Dorothy L. Williams recently interviewed 80 members of the United States Congress about the extent of which religion influenced their congressional voting behavior. Of those interviewed, 24 percent said that religious beliefs were a major influence upon their voting, 56 percent said that they were a moderate influence, 19 percent said that they were a minor influence, and only 1 percent said that religion was of no influence. Those who were identified as political liberals were just as likely to say that religion was a major or a moderate influence on their voting as were political conservatives. Republicans were as likely to claim religion as a major or moderate influence as were Democrats. (Peter L. Benson and Dorothy L. Williams, *Religion on Capitol Hill: Myths and Realities*, Oxford University Press, 1986, p. 143.)

Benson and Williams also questioned the Congressmen about their religious beliefs. Using cluster analysis, the interviewers identified six major types of religious beliefs held by the members. Of those sampled, 15 percent held a religious belief that was defined as "Legalistic." These members of Congress saw God as a lawgiver and saw religion as imposing discipline on their lives. Religion was a source of stability for these members' lives. Another group, about one third of those sampled, was devoted to a faith that was almost completely concerned with the relationship between the individual believer and God. Little concern was evidenced for others. This group, labeled the "Self-Concerned Religionists," saw God as a source of individual comfort and solace. About one seventh of the sample saw religious beliefs as a personally liberating force that gave them the freedom to speak and act. Their goal was not to please people but to act in accord with their conscience and thus to comply with their perception of God's wishes. That group was defined as being "Integrated Religionists." About 10 percent were defined as being "People-Concerned Religionists." They had an intense conviction that religious beliefs should move one to action and that such action should largely result in responding to the needs of the oppressed and the have-nots. Another group, 9 percent of the sample, were described as being "Nontraditional Religionists." These are people whose God is abstract, not a personal being, but a force or spirit or some even more uncertain concept. God to the "Nontraditionalist" is often a distant and impersonal force, even though "Nontraditionalists" may have had intense personal religious experiences. Slightly more than one fifth of the members in the sample were classified as being "Nominal Religionists." They show little enthusiasm for most religious themes. One may suspect that this group, more than any other, maintains church membership as a social or political expedient rather than as a personal dedication of faith. These six religious types cover a wide range of religious denominations. Benson and Williams argued that the reason previous studies of Congress did not find meaningful results was that they examined the relationship between denominations of the members of Congress and voting behavior. However, a member's denomination, unlike these categories of religion, does not identify how the religious message is received and internalized by the members. (*Ibid.*, pp. 123 – 139.) Table 2 shows that when these six religious beliefs are correlated with congressional voting behavior, clear patterns emerge. On issues such as "Pro-Civil Liberties," "Pro-Foreign Aid," "Pro-Hunger Relief," "Pro-Funding for Abortion," "Anti-Government Spending," "Pro-Strong Military," "Pro-Private Ownership," and "Pro-Free Enterprise," the People-Concerned Religionists and the Nontraditional Religionists are the first and second most liberal. The Legalistic Religionists and the Self-Concerned Religionists are the fifth and sixth most liberal, while the middle ground is taken by Integrated Religionists, who always rank third, and the Nominal Religionists, who always rank fourth. (*Ibid.*, p. 162.) If religious denominations of Congressmen tell us little about their voting behavior, religion as it is experienced in their lives tells us a great deal about how the Congressmen vote. To put it another way, the argument that the religious and secular experiences of those in public life are dichotomies—this a basic tenet of the thinking of strict separationists—is not borne out by this research.

Judicial Selection and Judicial Decisionmaking

One would think that at least the courts, as the protectors of the Constitution, would adhere to separationist thinking. However, Frank Sorauf's classic study of church and state litigation shows both the heavy involvement of religious groups in using the courts to forward their objectives and the im-

TABLE 2

Six Religious Types and Voting

Voting Behavior	Legalistic Religionists		Self-Concerned Religionists		Integrated Religionists		People-Concerned Religionists		Nontraditional Religionists		Nominal Religionists	
	Average*	Rank†	Average	Rank	Average	Rank	Average	Rank	Average	Rank	Average	Rank
Pro-Civil Liberties	32	5	30	6	60	3	80	2	81	1	51	4
Pro-Foreign Aid	21	6	26	5	63	3	97	1	88	2	55	4
Pro-Hunger Relief	30	5	29	6	78	3	90	1	83	2	60	4
Pro-Funding for Abortion	23	6	28	5	71	3	87	1	86	2	44	4
Anti-Government Spending	47	6	45	5	25	3	23	2	22	1	34	4
Pro-Strong Military	84	6	78	5	44	3	19	1	26	2	58	4
Pro-Private Ownership	50	5	54	6	29	3	19	2	18	1	37	4
Pro-Free Enterprise	65	6	61	5	35	3	23	2	20	1	42	4

* Refers to the percentage of the time that members in a given type vote in accordance with Voting Behavior measures.

† Represents the rank order of the 6 religious types, with 1 designating the most liberal type on the issue and 6 the most conservative.

Source: Peter L. Benson and Dorothy L. Williams, *Religion on Capitol Hill: Myths and Realities*, Oxford University Press, 1986, p. 161.

portance of religion in judicial decisionmaking (Frank Sorauf, *The Wall of Separation: The Constitutional Politics of Church and State*, Princeton University Press, 1976.) While the American Civil Liberties Union is well-known for espousing a separationist philosophy, the activities of groups with strong religious overtones are less known. The three major groups are the American Jewish Congress, Americans United for Separation of Church and State, and the Roman Catholic Church. Americans United and the American Jewish Congress have separationist goals, much like those of the American Civil Liberties Union. On the other hand, the Roman Catholic Church pursues accommodationist objectives. As a result, on church and state questions, a Protestant- and a Jewish-based organization frequently find themselves the adversaries of the Catholic Church.

The extent to which religiously based organizations use the judicial process to forward group goals on the church and state question is seen in Sorauf's analysis of 67 church and state cases decided between 1951 and 1971. They represent the universe of such cases decided during this period by the highest appellate court in a state, by the U.S. Courts of Appeals, or by the U.S. Supreme Court. (*Ibid.*, p. 371.) The three most active separationist groups involved in this litigation were the American Civil Liberties Union, the American Jewish Congress, and Americans United for Separation of Church and State. To a much lesser degree, the Seventh-Day Adventists, Southern Baptists, The Baptist Joint Committee, and the National Council of Churches were also involved in separationist litigation. Of the 67 cases, the American

Jewish Congress was involved in 22, and Americans
United for Separation of Church and State was involved in 30. Overall, Catholic interests, which were
overwhelmingly accommodationist on church and
state issues, were involved in 39 of the cases. (*Ibid*,
pp. 31–61.)

Religious interests are also strongly represented in
another aspect of the judicial process. Sorauf found a
strong relationship between the religion of the judge
and whether he or she decided cases from a separationist or an accommodationist perspective. Jewish
judges were the most strongly separationist, and
Catholic judges were the most accommodationist.
Protestant judges, in particular, tended to be more
separationist if Roman Catholic interests were involved in cases. (*Ibid.*, pp. 223–225.) Table 3 divides
the votes of judges in nonunanimous cases into
separationist and accommodationist positions. It then
identifies whether Roman Catholic interests are
present and identifies the judge by his or her religion.

That other studies have been less conclusive in
establishing a relationship between religion and judicial decisionmaking may be because the issues treated
were so broad that there was not strong religious interest in them. It may also be that religion was im-
properly measured—that is, other researchers used
religious affiliation as the key variable, rather than
using Benson and Williams' method of measuring
religiosity. Even in a straightforward correlational
study, however—one that tried to identify correlations between religious affiliation and "liberalism" or
"conservatism" of judges—Stuart Nagel found that
Catholic judges were to a statistically significant

TABLE 3

Votes by Religion of Judges in Nonunanimous Appellate Cases by Presence or Absence of Roman Catholic Interests in Cases

Votes in Nonunanimous Appellate Cases	Roman Catholic Interests Present				Roman Catholic Interests Not Present			
	Jewish	*Conservative Protestant*	*Other Protestant*	*Roman Catholic*	*Jewish*	*Conservative Protestant*	*Other Protestant*	*Roman Catholic*
Separationist	10 (76.9%)	16 (61.5%)	32 (44.4%)	2 (8.3%)	4 (100%)	7 (46.7%)	23 (56.1%)	3 (37.5%)
Accommodationist	3 (23.1%)	10 (38.5%)	40 (55.6%)	22 (91.7%)	0	8 (53.3%)	18 (43.9%)	5 (62.5%)
Total (N = 203):	13	26	72	24	4	15	41	8

Source: Frank J. Sorauf, *The Wall of Separation*, Princeton University Press, 1976, p. 225.

degree more likely to decide in favor of criminal
defendants on appeal, more likely to support government regulation of business, and more likely to rule in
favor of employees in workman's compensation cases.
In divorce cases, a strong correlation was found
between Catholicism of the judges and rulings in
favor of the wife. Interestingly, Catholics tended to be
Democrats and Protestants tended to be Republicans,
so there was a problem of determining whether the
differences between the Protestant and Catholic
judges was due to religion or to party affiliation.
(Stuart S. Nagel, "The Relationship Between the
Political and Ethnic Affiliation of Judges, and Their
Decision-Making," in Glendon Schubert, ed., *Judicial Behavior: A Reader in Theory and Research*,
Rand McNally, 1964, pp. 250 – 254.) Sheldon Goldman also found correlations between religion and
judicial decisionmaking of judges on the U.S. Courts
of Appeals. While the correlations were low, they
were statistically significant, indicating that Catholic
judges were more likely than Protestant judges to be
"economic liberals" and pro-injured party. (Sheldon
Goldman, "Voting Behavior on the United States
Court of Appeals Revisited," in Sheldon Goldman and
Austin Sarat, eds., *American Court Systems*, W. H.
Freeman, 1978, p. 401.) Kenneth Vines examined the
relationship between judicial decisionmaking and
race relations cases in the South from 1954 to 1962.
Classifying the judges according to their race relations decisions as "segregationist," "moderate," and
"integrationist," he found that those judges who did
not publicize their religious affiliation and those
judges who were Catholic tended to be "integra-

tionists." On the other hand, the orthodox Protestant judges tended to be either "segregationists" or "moderates." Vines suggested that the orthodox Protestants probably fit more closely into the Southern power structure than did Catholic judges or judges who did not publicize their affiliations. That closer fit to the power structure, suggested Vines, might explain the tendency for the orthodox Protestant judges to be less integrationist. (Kenneth N. Vines, "Federal District Judges and Race Relations Cases in the South," in Thomas P. Jahnige and Sheldon Goldman, eds., *The Federal Judicial System: Readings in Process and Behavior*, Dryden Press, 1968, pp. 134–135.) While conflicting findings have emerged which suggest no relationship between religion and judicial decisionmaking (e.g., Michael W. Giles and Thomas G. Walker, "Judicial Policy-Making and Southern School Segregation," in *American Court Systems*, p. 391), the above-mentioned studies do at least point to the strong possibility of a relationship between judges' religions and judges' voting behaviors in at least some issue areas.

Judicial selection is another area where there has not been total separation of church and state. There are times when the religion of judges has been an important factor in their selection. In the selection of Supreme Court Justices, for example, the popular wisdom is that there are a "Catholic seat" on the Court and a "Jewish seat" on the Court and that these seats are important in that they provide very visible representation to religious minorities and allow an appointing President to cultivate support from those minorities. As John Schmidhauser has pointed out, however, the importance of the notion of "Catholic seats" and "Jewish seats" on the Court has been greatly exaggerated. Evidence indicates that for appointing Presidents, the religion of Supreme Court nominees has tended to be a minor consideration, although Louis Brandeis's religion did play an important part in the problems he had in being confirmed for the Court. At most, religion seems to have played an important part only in the nominations of Felix Frankfurter, Frank Murphy, and William Brennan to the Court. Their appointments, however, do indicate that Presidents can and do use the religion of judicial nominees to cultivate votes from religious minorities. (John R. Schmidhauser, *Judges and Justices*, Little, Brown, 1979, pp. 62 – 68.)

While it may be understandable that in a separationist society, religious groups would sometimes battle for their interests in the legal process or that religion might be a consideration in a political appointment, the wall of separation should certainly apply, if it existed at all, to the influence of religion upon decisionmaking by judges.

Religion as a Political Lobby

No legal issue in the past twenty years has provoked an outcry equivalent to that initiated by the Court's decision in *Roe v. Wade*. (410 U.S. 113 [1973].) Opposition to *Roe* has had strong religious underpinnings from both conservative Protestants and Roman Catholics. Roman Catholics have, however, been more heavily involved in antiabortion activities. The typical pro-life activist outside the

South has been described as a Catholic housewife, who was probably educated in Catholic schools and is deeply religious and a regular churchgoer. She probably came from a large family and is the mother of several children. It is likely that this typical activist has never before been involved in political activity and was motivated to become so solely because of outrage over *Roe v. Wade*, which she sees as an attack upon motherhood, the role of women, and the purpose of sex. (Wald, p. 235.)

The role of such an activist must be seen in relation to the history of the opposition of the Catholic Church to abortion. There were inconsistencies in the Catholic Church's position on abortion during the long era that included Augustine of Hippo and Thomas Aquinas. Augustine did not believe that conception was the starting point of human life or that there was infusion of the soul at conception. Aquinas followed Aristotle's view that the fetus was unformed for males for forty days and for females for eighty days and that abortion before those times was not homicide. Of course, neither theologian had full awareness of the processes of conception. Neither, for example, was aware of the existence of ova. At least for these theologians, early abortion was not equivalent to murder, although they may have considered it morally wrong. By the time of Pope Sixtus V in 1588, abortion at any stage of pregnancy was grounds for excommunication. However, his successor, Pope Gregory XIV, more heavily influenced by Aristotle's views on conception, revoked all penalties for abortion in the first forty days of pregnancy. It was not until 1869 that the universal ban on abortion which was imposed by Pope Sixtus V was reimposed by Pope Pius IX. Pope Pius IX's position on abortion has been reenforced by Pope Paul VI's encyclical *Humanae Vitae* in 1968, by Vatican II, and in 1974 by the Sacred Congregation of the Doctrine. Thus, the position of the Church hierarchy has been strongly opposed to abortion since 1869, and the hierarchy emphasized that stand during the 1960s and 1970s. Although the condemnation of abortion has never been pronounced infallible and there has never been a pronouncement on when human life begins, the Vatican has taken such a strong antiabortion position that in 1986 it ordered Father Charles Curran, one of America's leading theologians and ethicists, to withdraw his teachings on abortion in which he argued that "abortion can be justified for preserving the life of the mother and for other important values commensurate with life" and that "there is no agreement about the morality of abortion among either philosophical or religious ethicists. . . ." (Patrick J. Sheeran, *Women, Society, the State, and Abortion: A Structuralist Analysis*, Praeger, 1987, pp. 81–83.)

The strength of the Church's position on abortion can be seen in the hierarchy's outcry after the *Roe* decision. Patrick Cardinal O'Boyle said that *Roe* was "a catastrophe for America." He also said that even though abortion was legal, it was not "morally permissible" but was "a hideous and heinous crime." Cardinal Cooke said, "Judicial decisions are not necessarily sound moral decisions," and "I hope and pray that our citizens will do all in their power to reverse this injustice to the rights of the unborn." Cardinal Krol said that *Roe* was "a monstrous injustice" and that "one trusts in the decency and good sense of the American people not to let an illogical court decision dictate to them on the subject of morality and human life." (Hyman Rodman, Betty Sarvis, and Joy Walker Bonar, *The Abortion Question*, Columbia University Press, 1987, pp. 104–105.)

Shortly after *Roe*, the American Catholic bishops created a lobbying organization, the National Committee for a Human Life Amendment. The goal was to pass a constitutional amendment which would reverse *Roe*. In 1974, the Senate Judiciary Committee held hearings on several proposed antiabortion amendments, and four Catholic bishops were among the many clergy who presented testimony. None of the 60 proposed amendments was sent to the floor of the Senate, so the Church began pursuing interim measures such as restrictions on abortion. (Wald, p. 232; Rodman, p. 109.) In 1975, the Catholic bishops developed the Pastoral Plan for Pro-Life Activities, which calls for the creation of pro-life organizations in every congressional district. It was envisioned that these organizations would have close ties to the Catholic Church and would provide money, campaign workers, and publicity for antiabortion candidates. These organizations have often gained a reputation for political clout, and a number of restrictions on abortions may be at least partly ascribed to their activities. Among these restrictions are mandatory waiting periods for abortions and spousal or parental consent laws. While these laws have been struck down by the Court as barriers to the exercise of a fundamental right (e.g., in *Planned Parenthood v. Danforth*, 428 U.S. 52 [1976]), antiabortionists successfully placed restrictions on the use of Medicaid funds, military insurance and federal employee insurance, and District of Columbia and foreign assistance appropriations for abortions. Bans on abortion funds for the Agency for International Development and in 30 states are other successes of the antiabortion movement. (Wald, p. 233.)

Interestingly, the Church's activities in the antiabortion arena have led to considerable tensions between the hierarchy and Catholic public officials who have argued that there is a difference between public policy and private morality. The battles between Governor Mario Cuomo of New York and John Cardinal O'Connor over the abortion issue and Cuomo's support of abortion in spite of his Catholicism have probably been the most visible indications of tension between the Church's position and that of some of the Church's members involved in the state's policy apparatus. (Rodman, pp. 144–145.) In 1984, Representative Geraldine Ferraro was rebuked by Bishop John Malone, the head of the U.S. Catholic Conference, for indicating that her votes on abortion policy would not be influenced by her Catholicism. Cardinal O'Connor stated in a televised interview that he could not understand how a Catholic could vote in good conscience for a candidate who did not pledge to support restrictive abortion policies. Several bishops appeared at Reagan campaign rallies, and the criticism of Ferraro's views on abortion continued throughout the campaign. Republican spokesmen stressed that the Republican platform was close to the Catholic position on abortion and attempted to convert Catholics, who have a traditional allegiance to the Democratic Party, to the GOP. (Wald, p. 237.)

While influential Catholic political leaders like Edward Kennedy argued that the Church was violating the wall of separation and that it was improper to impose restrictive abortion policies on the nation, the Church continued its lobbying against abortion. The antiabortion activists were having influence in high places. President Reagan ran on a Republican platform that endorsed a constitutional amendment to ban abortion. Strongly pro-life activist Dr. C. Everett Koop was named Surgeon General. In 1982, Reagan wrote nine Senators in support of Senator Jesse Helms's antiabortion activities and asked them for "an opportunity for the Supreme Court to reconsider its usurpation of the role of legislators and state courts" and to support "the humanity of the unborn." Before the Knights of Columbus in the same year, he said, "The national tragedy of abortion on demand must end." In 1985, the Justice Department filed an amicus brief supporting restrictions on abortion in Illinois and Pennsylvania and asking the Court to overturn its *Roe* decision. Reagan spoke in 1985 and 1986 to thousands of pro-lifers at the annual demonstration against *Roe v. Wade*. At the National Right to Life Convention in 1986, he described abortion as the "ultimate human rights issue." (Rodman, pp. 130–131.) Most important, it was claimed that opposition to *Roe v. Wade* was a "litmus test" imposed by the Reagan Administration on candidates for federal judgeships. (Aaron Freiwald, "The Mission: Stock Bench," in Jill Abramson, ed., *Reagan Justice: A Conservative Legacy on the Appellate Courts*, American

Lawyer Newspapers, 1988, p. 8.) Nor does the success of the antiabortion lobby seem limited to the Reagan Administration: then-Vice-President Bush also expressed his opposition to abortion on numerous occasions during the presidential campaign of 1988, although his rhetoric is often of a more cautious nature than President Reagan's.

Meanwhile, the Catholic Church has continued to engage in political activities over the abortion issue. A typical example is a form distributed in Dallas-area Catholic churches this October, "Respect Life Month" in the Roman Catholic Church, which solicited support for an amendment to the U.S. Constitution which would recognize constitutionally protected human life as beginning at conception. The form solicited the name, address, and phone number of the church member. It also had check-off spaces to determine whether the member was willing to receive the National Committee for a Human Life Amendment's newsletter, write his or her elected representative, visit his or her elected representative, or volunteer to help the cause in some other way. The petition on the form urged:

"The unborn, infants and the elderly should be protected. I am opposed to abortion, infanticide and euthanasia. Please add my name to the list of those supporting life, the LIFE ROLL, and advise my elected representatives and candidates for office of my pro-life position, and my support for a Human Life Amendment to the United States Constitution and all pro-life legislation that will protect and support human life rather than destroy it. And please keep me informed on how I can help support other pro-life activities."

Leading Catholic clergy are also attempting to tie the abortion issue to other aspects of the Church's agenda. Joseph Cardinal Bernardin, for example, has recently argued that while abortion is an issue that demands "*immediate* attention" (his emphasis), "we must be consistent in our support of all of life's issues." As a result, argued the cardinal, we should oppose abortion and euthanasia, work to prevent teenage suicide, oppose pornography, work against hunger, oppose capital punishment, and stop the nuclear arms race because "wherever life suffers, Jesus suffers." (Joseph Cardinal Bernardin, "Reflections on the Dignity of Human Life," a pamphlet distributed by the National Conference of Catholic Bishops, 1988.)

The political agenda of the Catholic Church, especially as it relates to abortion, has created a major constitutional issue which will probably be heard by the Supreme Court. For the past six years, the Catholic Church and proabortion activists have been sparring over issues of standing, the scope of discovery, and the jurisdiction of a federal district court. Eventually, the courts probably will have to resolve the core issue of whether the Catholic Church can maintain its Internal Revenue Service tax exemption as a charitable and educational institution and continue to engage in political activities relating to the antiabortion movement. (The major opinions in this chain of litigation include *Abortion Rights Mobilization* [hereafter cited as ARM] *v. Regan*, 544 F. Supp. 471 [1982]; *ARM v. Regan*, 552 F. Supp. 364 [1982]; and *ARM v. Regan*, 603 F. Supp. 970 [1985]. Most recently, see *U.S. Catholic Conference v. ARM*, 108 S. Ct. 2268 [1988].) It will be interesting to see how the Supreme Court, for it is surely a case that begs to be heard by the Court, will ultimately resolve this issue, which raises the question: Can the state use tax laws to discourage churches from addressing political questions that the churches see as religious questions? While I am exceedingly dubious that the state can do this, if it can, it would be the result of a benighted effort to create a wall of separation. Walls, however, have two sides, and while one side of the wall is separating church from state, the other side would be a barrier to the free exercise of religion.

Concluding Remarks

I have emphasized that separation of church and state is impossible in the American political context, where religion is a major interest of Americans and where there is significant overlap between matters of religious faith and matters of public policy. Again, I would stress that the myth of separation is nevertheless important and that it likely reduces some religious tensions in America and prevents some of the more extreme efforts to create late-twentieth-century equivalencies of a state church. However, separation is a myth and not a reality in the American political system. Regardless of what the framers may have felt, the language of the Constitution, or the verbiage of the Supreme Court, religion plays a central part in public policy and in public life, as the above illustrations—a handful of many possible illustrations of the interaction between religion and the state—have pointed out.

It should also be stressed, contrary to some journalistic accounts of the activities of the Religious Right in America during the 1980s, that the involvement of religion in American political life is nothing new. And the Republic can survive religion in that broad middle ground of American politics, whether it be Catholic mothers picketing abortion clinics, voters choosing a born-again Christian for the presidency, or baby Jesus in a city-owned manger being watched over by Santa Claus. After all, as the latter-day strict separationist William O. Douglas once wrote in what Justice Jackson considered one of Douglas's more "evangelistic" moments (*Zorach v. Clauson*, 72 S. Ct. 679, 689 [1952]), "We are a religious people." (*Ibid.*, 684.)

FROM CIVIL RELIGION
TO PUBLIC FAITH

by

George Erik Rupp

George Erik Rupp

George Rupp became Rice University's fifth president on July 1, 1985. Prior to his appointment at Rice, Dr. Rupp had been a faculty member and administrator at Johnston College in the University of Redlands (California), at the University of Wisconsin-Green Bay, and at Harvard, where he was John Lord O'Brian Professor of Divinity and Dean of the Divinity School.

Dr. Rupp's undergraduate major was in German and English literature at the University of Munich in Germany and Princeton University, where he was awarded the A.B. degree and Phi Beta Kappa in 1964. He was awarded the B.D. (Bachelor of Divinity) degree in 1967 from Yale and the Ph.D. from Harvard in 1971.

Following receipt of his doctorate and his ordination the same year as a minister in the Presbyterian Church, Dr. Rupp served as Faculty Fellow in religion at Johnston College, the exprimental unit of the University of Redlands in Redlands, California. In 1973 he was appointed vice chancellor of Johnston College.

In 1974 Dr. Rupp returned to Harvard University and its Divinity School, first as assistant professor of theology and, in 1976, as associate professor and chairperson of the department of theology. While at Harvard he served as associate editor of the Harvard Theological Review *and became founding co-editor of the* Harvard Dissertations in Religion *series.*

In 1977 Dr. Rupp was appointed professor of humanistic studies and Dean for Academic Affairs at the University of Wisconsin, Green Bay.

As Dean of the Harvard Divinity School beginning in 1979, Dr. Rupp led the school in curriculum revision, enhancement of programs in women's studies in religion, and creation of programs in Christian-Jewish relations and medicine and religion.

President Rupp is the author of three books: Christologies and Cultures: Toward a Typology of Religious Worldviews *(1974);* "Culture-Protestantism": German Liberal Theology at the Turn of the Twentieth Century *(1977); and* Beyond Existentialism and Zen: Religion in a Pluralistic World *(1979). He is also the author of numerous articles in professional journals.*

FROM CIVIL RELIGION TO PUBLIC FAITH

by

George Rupp

In this paper, I will delineate what I consider the most promising approach to the issues involved in the relationship between religious and political life. I will proceed as follows. First, I will offer my assessment of the general project pointed to with the term "civil religion." I use this term to refer to attempts to express a shared set of religious values in order to provide a common frame of reference for society as a whole. Because I find such attempts instructive even when the lessons are as much negative as positive, I will conduct an audit of what I take to be the assets and the liabilities of civil religion in this sense. Against the background of this balance sheet, I will, secondly, describe and evaluate the alternative to civil religion represented in appeals to the absolute authority of religious experience or revealed truth. Here, too, I will attempt to identify weaknesses as well as strengths. Thirdly, I will sketch a chastened approach to civil religion that I term "public faith." In elaborating this approach I will seek to appropriate the strengths of both civil religion and its critics while guarding against their weaknesses. Fourthly and finally, I will offer an overview of the implications of this position for current debates about the relationship of religion to politics.

Civil Religion

The assets or strengths or virtues of civil religion are considerable. I note two in particular: civil religion is intentionally public in character; and it represents an attempt to identify common ground among positions that may differ in significant particulars. Both of these virtues are impressive, and in American civil religion they mutually support and reinforce each other. But despite their close association here, they are in principle separable and not infrequently separate in other contexts.

In the history of virtually all human societies, the public character of religion has been simply taken for granted. What has come to be called religion was the shared system of symbolic forms and acts, the myths and rituals, that interpreted and in turn shaped personal identity, social institutions, and cultural patterns. Such a system of symbols was pervasively present in public life even when it was not a focus of general awareness. In a culturally homogeneous traditional society, a common system of symbolic forms and acts provided the shared frame of reference for that society. But even when there was a recognized plurality of religious and cultural communities, by far the most common pattern in human history has been for a single tradition to occupy the position of the officially sanctioned religion. In short, religion has been publicly established—either as the taken-for-granted frame of reference of all members of the society or as the dominant religious position, in effect the religious counterpart of political authority, supported by the state and in turn providing legitimation for that state.

The institutionalization of religion in America stands in sharp contrast to this prevailing pattern in human history. The situation here is certainly not without significant antecedents and precedents. In particular, the American experiment is derived from two central developments of the European Reformation and Enlightenment: first, the splintering of Western Christendom into a plurality of distinct churches; and second, the growth of an intellectual tradition self-consciously critical of all the forms of ecclesiastical Christianity. But the American experiment does more than simply replicate or perpetuate this double inheritance. Instead it expresses the implications of this pluralism and criticism in institutional terms. The result is the American rejection in principle of an established national church—in contrast both to homogeneous traditional cultures and to societies that accord privileged or official status to only one or two religious communities.

This context of disestablishment of religion is what renders the intentionally public character of civil religion noteworthy. In societies in which religion is established, its public character may go without saying. But when religion is in principle not officially sanctioned and when multiple religious communities not only coexist but are defined as having equal societal status and when, finally, a tradition of criticism of all religion is socially accepted, then the intentionally public character of religion is an attainment rather than a given.

This attainment must resist and overcome the temptations inherent in this context to construe religion in simply privatized terms. The forms of religion that succumb to this temptation are much in evidence: religion is only a matter of personal taste or preference, salvation has to do only with individual fulfillment either here and now or in the beyond hereafter, and so on. Over against such privatized interpretations of religious symbolism, civil religion insists on a role in shaping the values that undergird public life and in promoting a sense of social responsibility that transcends the interests of the individual. That, then, is a central strength of civil religion: its intentionally public character.

The second of the two virtues I note is the commitment of civil religion to identifying common ground among differing particular positions. The pluralism involved has certainly broadened and deepened over time. Among the founders of the country, the range of positions taken into account was quite limited. Even radicals like Tom Paine were still strongly under Christian influence in arguing for a kind of unitarian deism. The commitment in principle against every national establishment of religion, however, not only protected other Christians against Anglicans or Calvinists but also set the precedent for the protection of a host of other communities—including in particular Jews (and now also Buddhists, Hindus, Muslims, and others)—and also of course for so-called nonbelievers of all kinds.

In this context of increasingly radical pluralism, the attempt to discern common ground among quite different positions is enormously difficult but nonetheless unavoidable. To identify, express, and affirm shared values in and through quite different symbolic forms is a challenge that must be faced if a genuinely pluralistic society is to develop a workable polity. Accordingly, the commitment of civil religion to this task of fashioning and sustaining the fundamental values and institutional patterns common to the society as a whole is a significant strength.

As much as this discerning of common ground in and through differences may be an asset, however, it also points to liabilities in civil religion. Two are especially worth noting. The first is that in seeking common ground, civil religion too often reduces distinctive traditions to a least common denominator. The second is that in struggling to articulate fundamental values and institutional patterns for the society as a whole, civil religion may become an uncritical apologist for existing arrangements.

The first liability scarcely needs elaboration. Most of us are all too familiar with the pallid fare that results when religious commitments are reduced to a least common denominator. Think of the average council of churches or interfaith worship service. Such organizations and events no doubt serve definite purposes. But they are scarcely religiously vital or dynamic. Instead they are frankly derivative and therefore unavoidably dependent on the particular communities being brought together. In attempting to encompass a wide range of ideas and attitudes, civil religion is always in danger of sacrificing the depth of particular commitment.

The second liability similarly follows from the attempt to be encompassing or inclusive. In seeking to express overall affirmations, civil religion may submerge minority positions or obscure underrepresented interests. In providing a sacred canopy for society as a whole, civil religion too often legitimates only established ideational traditions and social arrangements. Although underlying values and institutional commitments may have the potential for registering criticism of and even resistance to prevailing patterns, this potential is not realized, because of the actual power of established interests to shape the acceptable forms of civil religion. Indeed, because civil religion is not solidly grounded in particular religious communities, it may all too readily be appropriated and manipulated by political leaders seeking to provide legitimation for their own agenda.

To summarize, here then is the balance sheet on civil religion as I have outlined it. On the positive side, there are two assets: first, civil religion is intentionally public in character; and, second, it seeks common ground among diverse positions. And on the negative side, there are two liabilities: first, civil religion may attain breadth at the expense of depth; and, second, it may lead to an erosion of the critical power of religious commitment over the broader society. Against the background of this balance sheet, it is scarcely surprising that there is ambivalence about civil religion and that the quest for alternatives is both recurrent and persistent.

Absolute Claim

To counter the tendency of religion or theology to become subservient to the prevailing culture, religious individuals and communities characteristically appeal to the authority of religious insight or revelation. In its sharpest form, this appeal is to the unqualified or absolute authority of religious insight or revealed truth over against which all other standards are deemed decisively limited, inadequate, deficient, even perverse. Especially for those religious communities with a strong prophetic tradition, the attractions of standing staunchly against established practice are quite strong. Those attractions are certainly resistible: even religious communities with strong prophetic traditions have all too frequently managed to ignore them in favor of accommodations with the prevailing culture. Still, appeal to an unassailable authority standing in judgment against the dominant tendencies of the broader society imbues religious commitment with a heady sense of purpose and an impressive social and cultural power. To thunder "Thus saith the Lord" or to assert "The Bible says" or to pronounce a practice to be a "sin against the law of God" is to assume intrinsic religious authority. Not surprisingly, such authoritative appeals are very attractive in comparison to settling for the situation into which civil religion may degenerate—namely, the situation in which religious traditions provide only ornaments for a secular mass culture and consumer society. In contrast to this trap, religion based on appeal to unassailable authority has the double attraction of being both irreducibly particular and forcefully critical.

Probably the best-known twentieth-century instance of such criticism in Christian traditions is the 1934 Barmen Declaration, in which a federation of churches in Germany protested against the pretensions of Nazism. This eloquent confession is often cited as evidence of the prophetic power of appeals to divine revelation. It may, accordingly, be worth taking note of this instance in some detail.

The Barmen Declaration admirably exemplifies how religious authority that is sharply distinguished from secular culture may be invoked in opposition to the prevailing trends of that culture. In short, the Barmen Declaration expressed an eloquent and potent No! to its age. It articulated that rejection through appeal to sharply stated Christian confessions. The confessions were formulated as interpretations of specific verses from the Bible. Each verse is from the New Testament and was selected to authorize absolute and exclusive claims for Christ and the Christian church. The resultant affirmation in each case was in turn contrasted with what is rejected as false doctrine. Included in particular was the rejection of every claim that "events and powers, figures and truths" other than "the one Word of God" are "God's revelation." Also rejected was the attempt either to imbue the church with secular power or to arrogate to the state the role of "the single and total order of human life, thus fulfilling the church's vocation as well." ("Barmen Theological Declaration" in Rolf Ahlers, *The Barmen Theological Declaration of 1934: The Archaeology of a Confessional Text*, The Edwin Mellon Press, 1986, pp. 39–42; the specific phrases quoted are on pp. 40 and 42.)

As is evident from even this very cursory summary, the critical power of the Barmen Declaration was generated through appeals to the authority of the Word of God and the highly particular identity of the Christian church as differentiated from the broader culture. This critical power was enormously important. It represents the all-too-infrequent prophetic stance of religious truth over against the perversity of the secular or quasi-religious world. As such, it is an enduring testimony to the capacity of religious commitment to stand against, to resist, the idolatry of every human authority that claims to be ultimate.

And yet even in and through the eloquence of testimony against the idolatry of human ideologies like Nazism, the limitations of this stance are also evident. Precisely because of the sharply focused particularity of its appeal, the Barmen Declaration was notably deficient in addressing issues beyond the assertion of the authority and the autonomy of the Christian church. The interests of the church were firmly registered. In allowing themselves to be co-opted by the Third Reich, the so-called German Christians were attacked for undermining the integrity of the Christian church. This hybrid of state and church was, therefore, to be resisted with the uncompromising fervor that grounding in the truth of revelation provided. The result was the assertion of the autonomous authority of the church of Christ—the federation of German Confessional Churches, Lutheran, Reformed, and United, bound together in this declaration of the German Evangelical Church. But beyond the assertion of the autonomy of this Evangelical Church, the Barmen Declaration was notably silent about other issues. Here the exclusive reliance on verses from the New Testament is indicative. Perhaps to avoid dissension within the various Protestant Christian communities, no appeal to the Hebrew scriptures was included. Nor was there any condemnation of the increasingly blatant anti-Semitism of

the Third Reich. Instead, the Barmen Declaration
confined itself to appeals to the authorities of particular Christian communities and asserted the
autonomy of the Christian church over against the so-
called German Christian churches and their govern-
ment-supported administrators.

Even in and through its eloquent testimony against
the idolatrous glorification of secular or quasi-
religious ideologies, the Barmen Declaration therefore illustrates inadequacies in the reliance upon
appeals to particular authorities that are in principle
alleged to be discontinuous with ordinary historical
experience. Such appeals do generate and conduct a
sense of power for particular individuals and communities that are under assault. Because of the sharp dis-
junction between the transcendent authority invoked
and the specific historical situation being threatened,
such appeals too often do not, however, provide positive guidance for historical action outside the
boundaries of the community whose interests and
identity are being preserved.

Illustrations of this pattern are not, of course, confined to the Barmen Declaration and the theology
associated with it. Instead, the pattern is a recurrent
one across religious traditions. In stark form, it is
illustrated in the discipline of ascetics, hermits, and
monks who turn from entanglements in this world to
focus on orientation to an ultimate reality at least distinguished from, if not opposed to, ordinary historical
life. Think of Taoist recluses, Hindu ascetics, early
Christian desert hermits, Theravada Buddhist or
Catholic Christian solitary monks. There are, of
course, also less austere examples of the pattern, as is

evident in the myriad instances in the history of religions of widely held views that so concentrate on the goal of salvation in another realm that their dominant attitude toward secular life is one of rejection. All such positions share a critical stance toward historical attainments. But they also share a lack of interest in or inclination for shaping, or a capacity to shape, historical life toward positive achievement or fulfillment.

To sum up, while appeals to the unqualified or absolute authority of religious insight or revelation are attractive because of the critical power that they generate and conduct, such appeals are also deeply problematical on two grounds. First, there is the threat of a retreat to private insight or exclusively particular awareness—a threat unavoidably entailed in the claim to have direct access to absolute truth, access which is in principle different from all other human experience and therefore discontinuous with such other experience and not subject to generally accepted modes of understanding and evaluation. Second, there is the more pragmatic problem that the impulse toward unqualified condemnation of society, and certainly even more the tendency toward undifferentiated rejection of the world, results in a lack of constructive guidance not substantially different from the effects of secular relativism.

Public Faith

In seeking to appropriate the strengths of both civil religion and its critics while guarding against their weaknesses, it is initially encouraging to note that

each position in fact has substantial resources for
countering the weaknesses of the other. The critical
power of appeals to the absolute authority of religious
experience or revealed truth offers a welcome contrast to the tendency in civil religion to be shallow and
uncritical. Conversely, the positive impulse of civil
religion in seeking to be public in character and to
identify common ground among differing positions
provides an orientation that programmatically resists
the tendency of authoritarian religion to retreat to
private appeals that deliver too little publicly accessible guidance for historical life, especially in pluralistic societies.

While the respective strengths of civil religion and
its critics are evident and also evidently in each case
offer correctives to the weaknesses of the other, the
strengths themselves are not, however, self-evidently
compatible. The critical power of particular religious
conviction over the broader society derives in significant measure from its very particularity in insisting on
the authority of truth that is not accessible through
the methods of, or in keeping with, the canons of ordinary knowing. Accordingly, this strength of the critical power of particular religion is not incidentally but
rather systematically opposed to the positive impulses
of civil religion in seeking to be public and to affirm
common ground among different positions.

The central question to be addressed in attempting
to sketch a chastened approach to civil religion is,
therefore, how commitment may be both particular
and public—how it may seek common ground in the
public arena while at the same time generating and
conducting the critical power of particular religion.

This question is of more than only theoretical interest. In an era which is witnessing serious erosion of consensus about common or shared values, it also assumes great practical import, as is evident in debates concerning the role of religion in political life.

Commitment that is both particular and public in principle rejects the two easiest and probably most frequent resolutions of the tensions entailed in this set of issues. It rejects the reduction of religion to a least common denominator allegedly shared by all. At the same time, it refuses to confine religion to the private sphere. In this double rejection, public faith parts company both with religious liberals who advocate toleration as a sufficient response to pluralism and with secular humanists who prefer to keep religion altogether out of such domains as economics and politics.

The distinctiveness of public faith so construed is perhaps most evident in the ways it exercises critical power over the broader society. It may appeal to the particular traditions of its own community—its stories or teachings or injunctions. But it recognizes that those traditions are not authoritative apart from their capacity to illuminate and their power to shape public issues that confront adherents and nonadherents alike. This requirement of accessibility to others does not mean that only common or shared traditions may be appropriately invoked. It does, however, preclude the imposition of standards or obligations that are advocated exclusively on the basis of appeals to allegedly absolute authorities.

The critical power of appeals to religious authority derives from their claim to represent transcendent

truth over against the ways of the world. Hence, even
when those appeals are expressed in highly particular
forms, they invoke the authority of universal truth.
Analogously, insofar as civil religion is critical, it
appeals to norms or principles or ideals that inform
but also transcend the best practice of a given society.
In this case as well, there is reference to transcending
value or universal truth. Public faith also enlists this
power of appeal to the transcendent and the universal. But it does so with greater awareness of the
need for leverage against the characteristic provincialisms to which civil religion and religious authoritarianism are prone.

The provincialism to which civil religion is inclined
results from its tendency to reflect, and in turn to
legitimate, the values of the society for which it
provides a general frame of reference. Because civil
religion attempts to identify common ground among
positions that may differ in significant particulars, it is
in intention less provincial than the traditions among
which it mediates. For example, insofar as American
civil religion succeeds in articulating values shared by
Protestants of many denominations and perhaps also
by Catholics and Jews, it at least initially seems less
provincial than, say, humanist (as distinguished from
theist and Christian) Unitarian-Universalism or
Trappist monasticism or Hassidic Judaism. But this intention to be inclusive in one or more respects may
too easily obscure the provincialism inherent in the
very attempt to provide a frame of reference for one
specific society, in this case the United States of
America. In sum, the aim of encompassing several
religious traditions within a single nation in effect

accentuates the features of the national identity that those religious traditions have in common.

Unlike civil religion, appeals to the absolute authority of religious experience or revealed truth have no intrinsic or necessary relationship to a single society or nation. Such appeals are not intrinsically provincial in a geographical sense. Indeed, great missionary religions—Buddhism, Christianity, and Islam, to take the three most powerful instances in human history—have a universalistic thrust that is a substantial resource for countering every such geographical provincialism. But precisely this universalizing missionary thrust in turn entails the threat of its own provincialism: a cultural or symbolic provincialism rather than a natural or geographical one. This provincialism results from the presumption of direct access to absolute truth, access typically (though not invariably) restricted to those who attain the same standpoint or follow the same approach and interpret that standpoint or approach with reference to the same set of symbols.

Public faith must resist both the national provincialism of civil religion and the cultural provincialism of religious authoritarianism. It can do so by building on the sound instincts that both civil religion and appeals to the absolute authority of particular religions have in countering their own characteristic provincialisms. But it can then also reinforce those positive tendencies by affirming the criticism that each has of the other.

Civil religion at its best guards against the threat of national idolatry through appeals to transcending value or universal truth that stands in judgment over

the pretensions and the collective self-interest of the
nation. Thus even civil religion is not without its
prophets. The figure of Abraham Lincoln—perhaps
the foremost exemplar of American civil religion—is
eloquent testimony to this capacity for national self-
criticism in civil religion. So there are resources
within the traditions of civil religion for countering
the tendency toward uncritical glorification of the nation. Because public faith is not committed to seeking
a least common denominator, it may, however, also invoke the particular traditions of its own community,
specifically including commitments to a universalism
that transcends every provincial society, as a further
reinforcement of resistance to national idolatries of
every sort. Thus, despite disagreements on other
grounds, public faith shares with authoritarian
religion the capacity to appeal to highly particular
traditions that are universal in scope and therefore
relativize the absolutist pretensions of any single
nation.

This capacity to resist the human temptation to self-
glorification is a great strength of particular religion.
Too often this critical capacity is not, however, extended to rigorous self-criticism. The result is an
absolutizing of one historically relative tradition of interpretation in one religious community and an insistence that this authoritative position may not
appropriately be subjected to critical and comparative
scrutiny. At this point, public faith parts company
with authoritarian religion. It maintains that every
position, including its own, must in principle allow for
the most uncompromising criticism (including especially self-criticism) and comparative assessment.

Through such public interchange with other communities, the characteristic provincialism of authoritarian religion—namely its tendency toward absolutizing its own perspective—may be countered. And only on the basis of such public interaction among multiple religious as well as secular communities may increasingly adequate expressions of public faith be developed in a pluralistic world.

Public faith may, then, be both particular and public only because it is also committed to critical and comparative inquiry. Through critical and comparative interaction with its counterparts in both religious and secular traditions, public faith seeks more adequate expressions of its own commitments. At the same time, the relative adequacy of its diagnoses and prescriptions is the basis on which it commends its positions. This relative adequacy in interpreting and, in turn, in shaping an increasingly shared global experience is the authority to which particular commitment appeals in the public arena—an authority that provides a common court of appeal for all such particular claims.

Religion and Politics

I am aware that this sketch of public faith is at a sufficiently high level of abstraction that it may seem quite removed from actual debates about the appropriate role of religion in civic affairs. I will, therefore, conclude with a brief overview of how I see the implications of this conception of public faith for the relationship of religion to politics, implications which will provide a final set of contrasts of both civil religion and religious authoritarianism.

The conception of public faith as I have sketched it implies a twofold principle to guide reflection on the relationship of religion and politics. First, government should in no way whatsoever either support or suppress specific religious positions as such. Second, religiously committed individuals and institutions should be entirely free to participate in whatever ways they choose in the full range to political expression and organization. This formulation is deliberately asymmetrical: there should be a wall of separatism between church and state, but it should block traffic in only one direction. Put less metaphorically, while government should not interfere with religious life, religion can and should shape political deliberations.

Pressure to transgress the first tenet of this twofold principle is exerted from various quarters. Civil religion violates it insofar as it tends not only to align a common religious orientation with the political order but also to enlist government in support of specific religious positions. But so, too, do religious communities that seek government sanction for their particular views. The issue of prayer in the public schools of the United States illustrates this tendency— whether it is a quite particular prayer, like the Lord's Prayer, or a very general prayer that might be said by at least some Hindus, Muslims, and Jews, as well as Christians. In either case, enlisting state support for religious observance transgresses the first tenet of this twofold principle, to the disservice of religion as well as of politics.

As for the second tenet, it simply recognizes how unacceptable it is to religiously committed people to expect that their deepest convictions will not influence their political behavior. To insist that individuals and institutions be free to participate in political life in whatever ways they deem appropriate does not entail approbation for any and every form of such participation. It does, however, recognize that religious individuals and institutions must themselves be allowed to determine the modes of participation they deem appropriate. So, for example, black churches may well continue their long-established practice of endorsing specific candidates for office and even of serving as a base for political organizing. Or, to take other instances, religious leaders are entirely free to express their views on the implications of their various traditions on such public issues as racial justice, appropriate health care, welfare funding, foreign aid, nuclear arms, and abortion.

This general formulation of the twofold principle that guides public faith in reflecting on the relationship of religion to politics still leaves a host of decisions unresolved as religious individuals and communities confront specific issues. But those unresolved decisions are properly located in the deliberations of religious communities rather than in the political process. It may be that most religious leaders and institutions are well-advised to resist endorsements of individual candidates. But that is a decision for them to make, not one to be forced on them through political disenfranchisement. Similarly, religious communities may decide against taking firm positions on public issues that are hotly contested and on which their own members are sharply divided. But this question also is one for religious communities themselves to decide.

There is no doubt that the presence of religion in public life can and usually does heighten the intensity of debate in ways that too often block resolution of pressing issues. The fact enhances the attractiveness of banning religion from the public arena. But the cost of completely privatizing religion is too high a price to pay for the benefit of greater tranquility in public affairs.

We are becoming more and more acutely aware of how costly it is to settle for public life divorced from the questions of meaning and value central to religious commitment. Influential religious and political leaders are prepared to trade in the currency that perhaps a majority of our fellow citizens accept as their own. The dangers of inadequate civil religion are, however, evident in such commerce: an uncritical celebration of the dominant traditions of the nation to the exclusion of critical or subordinated voices.

Over against this homogenizing and triumphalist tendency, what we need is public faith: commitment, whether religious or secular, that is unapologetically particular because it recognizes its roots in definite communities and traditions and values but that is also entirely public because it is committed to comparative and critical inquiry. That is a tall order. It certainly would be easier if we had a single set of symbols that all of us agreed were both rich and compelling. But that is not the case. Accordingly, nothing less than something like the tougher stance of public faith will do if we are to continue to have—or, perhaps better, to reestablish—a society with public purposes beyond individual gratification.

LOYALTY

by

Andrew R. Cecil

Andrew R. Cecil

Andrew R. Cecil is Distinguished Scholar in Residence at The University of Texas at Dallas. In February 1979 the University established in his honor the Andrew R. Cecil Lectures on Moral Values in a Free Society, and invited Dr. Cecil to deliver the first series of lectures in November 1979. The first annual proceedings were published as Dr. Cecil's book The Third Way: Enlightened Capitalism and the Search for a New Social Order, *which received an enthusiastic response. He has also lectured in each subsequent series. A new book,* The Foundations of a Free Society, *was published in 1983. Another,* Three Sources of National Strength, *appeared in 1986. In 1976, the University named for Dr. Cecil the Andrew R. Cecil Auditorium.*

Educated in Europe and well launched on a career as a professor and practitioner in the fields of law and economics, Dr. Cecil resumed his academic career after World War II in Lima, Peru, at the University of San Marcos. After 1949, he was associated with the Methodist church-affiliated colleges and universities in the United States until he joined The Southwestern Legal Foundation. Associated with the Foundation since 1958, Dr. Cecil helped guide its development of five educational centers that offer nationally and internationally recognized programs in advanced continuing education. Since his retirement as President of the Foundation, he serves as Chancellor Emeritus and Honorary Trustee.

Dr. Cecil is author of fifteen books on the subjects of law, economics, and religion and of more than seventy articles on these subjects and on the philosophy of religion published in periodicals and anthologies. A member of the American Society of International Law, of the American Branch of the International Law Association, and the American Judicature Society, Dr. Cecil has served on numerous commissions for the Methodist Church, and is a member of the Board of Trustees of the National Methodist Foundation for Christian Higher Education. In 1981 he was named an Honorary Rotarian.

LOYALTY

by

Andrew R. Cecil

The Concept of Loyalty

Loyalty is an ethical principle essential to moral life. It may be defined as a devotion to a cause marked by thoroughness, fidelity, constancy, a sense of just purpose, and a willingness to serve. It connotes faithfulness, a duty to serve, and an allegiance to some definite authority or cause—to God, to a person, to a constitution, to a principle, or to an idea. Loyalty is not merely an affection since it demands the willingness of the loyal person to serve and to be ready to suffer as the cause demands.

Loyalty is a virtue essential to democracy since it binds the members of a society by ties that lead to unity of purpose and solidarity in service. For the American philosopher Josiah Royce, "loyalty to loyalty" is the central spirit of the moral and reasonable life of man. All the commonplace virtues, insofar as they are indeed defensible and effective, are special forms of loyalty to loyalty. "Justice, charity, industry, wisdom, spirituality, are all definable in terms of enlightened loyalty." (*The Basic Writings of Josiah Royce*, Vol. 2, University of Chicago Press, 1969, p. 860. Reprinted from *The Philosophy of Loyalty*, The Macmillan Company, 1908.)

The history of loyalty, of serving a cause beyond
one's private self, is the history of human great-
ness—of patriots who regretted that they had but one
life to give to their country, of captains standing stead-
fastly by their sinking ships until the last possible
service could be rendered, of martyrs faithful to their
religions unto death, of political prisoners who died
tortured by their oppressors without betraying their
freedom-seeking friends.

The fact that loyalty is a central motive in an individual's life does not mean that it affects his independent judgment, his spirit of self-assertion, or his
moral autonomy. An individual's free judgment may
lead him to the conclusion that his blind loyalty has
been exploited for unworthy purposes. Immigrants to
the United States from totalitarian countries do not
hesitate to renounce their fidelity to their native
countries and to pledge loyalty to this country, which
offers them the right of self-expression and freedom
denied to them by the oppressors who trammeled
their free spirits.

A member of a political party disillusioned with the
leadership of the party and with the policies adopted
and consistently followed by it which conflict with his
political views and moral standards may reach the
conclusion that he cannot remain loyal to the ties that
bound him with the other members into some sort of
unity. Such a conclusion should not be interpreted as
a sign of weakness or lack of fidelity. It is, rather, a
sign of independence, of a refusal to become a tool in
the hands of others. It is a sign of the moral autonomy
of the individual, which Immanuel Kant insisted is

one of our highest goods. This moral autonomy should guide the individual in determining his loyalty to any civic or social organization, club, or fraternity.

Not all causes are worthy of loyalty. There are good and bad causes. Gangsters, mercenaries, and drug pushers also claim ties that bind them into one sort of action—criminal action. War, unless in defense against aggression, can hardly be considered a just cause. Yet loyalty has been closely associated with the activities of war. When aroused by the spirit of war, one is led to hate the enemy precisely because the enemy possesses the same personal quality of loyalty one admires in a countryman—only the enemy is loyal to a different group or cause. The ethnologist Dr. Rudolf Steinmetz of The Hague in his book *The Philosophy of War* maintained that warriors are the most typical representatives of rational loyalty. According to him, war gives an opportunity for loyal devotion so notable and important that, if war were altogether abolished, one of the greatest goods of civilization would be hopelessly lost. (Quoted in *The Basic Writings of Josiah Royce*, p. 859.)

Although it is more than doubtful whether wars do make a positive contribution to civilization, it cannot be denied that it is sometimes impossible to define what is right and what is wrong. The truth about right and wrong can be discovered only upon examination of the purpose of life. Throughout the history of mankind, prominent philosophers who have tried to discover the great truths of moral life have taken into account the importance of loyalty as one of the great virtues classifying the morality of human behavior.

Socrates, Plato, Aristotle, and Cicero

Loyalty was praised as a virtue and its importance stressed by the ancient Greek philosophers. Socrates, condemned to death, reaffirmed his loyalty to God, to Athens, and above all to his mission to "pursue wisdom" when Crito, among other Athenians, came to his cell to advise him that a way had been found for him to escape. If he were to have left his "post" because of fear of death, he said,

> "that would have been dreadful indeed, and then in truth might I be justly brought to court for not acknowledging the existence of gods, for willful disobedience to the oracle, for fearing death, for thinking myself wise when I am not." (*Apology*, 29a, trans. by R. E. Allen, *The Dialogues of Plato*, Vol. I, Yale University Press, 1984, p. 92.)

In his discussion with the Athenians who were visiting him in his cell, Socrates brought up the suggestion that had been made that the case against him would be dismissed on the condition that he no longer pursue his philosophy, his inquiry, and his teaching. Such conditions were in direct conflict with his loyalty to his mission:

> "If, as I say, you were to dismiss me on that condition, I would reply that I hold you in friendship and regard, Gentlemen of Athens, but I shall obey the God rather than you, and while I have breath and am able I shall not cease to pursue wisdom." (*Ibid.*, 29d.)

Socrates believed that God commanded him to persuade "young and old . . . to care not for body or money in place of, or so much as, excellence of soul." He showed himself determined to remain loyal to his true self and in his service to God, even if he had "to die for it many times over." By refusing to disobey the law and to escape, he remained loyal to the laws of the state, even if they were unjust. His choice was to die as "a victim of injustice at the hands of men" rather than to escape and trespass the law and "thus shamefully return injustice for injustice and injury for injury." (*Crito*, 54c, *The Dialogues of Plato*, p. 129.)

Plato and Aristotle both demanded unselfish loyalty and complete devotion to the city-state, the model form of social and political organization in which people participate in directing the affairs of the city (*polis*) and in making the laws. Plato in his *Laws* demanded the death penalty for any citizens found guilty of a crime committed against "the gods, or his parents, or the state." Whoever, he wrote, uses violence and is "stirring up sedition contrary to law" is the greatest enemy of the state. There should be one law for all three kinds of evildoer: "for the traitor, and the robber of temples, and the subverter by violence of the laws of the state." Every man who "is worth anything" has the obligation to inform the magistrate and "bring the conspirator to trial for making a violent and illegal attempt to change the government." The citizen who fails to discharge this obligation and the magistrate who does not suppress the man who stirs up civil strife are "nearly as bad" as the "subverter of the laws of the state." (*Laws IX*, trans.

by Benjamin Jowett, *The Dialogues of Plato*, Vol. 2, Random House, 1937, pp. 600, 602.)

Plato discerned two kinds of war. One was civil war, "of all wars the worst"; the other war, with foreign nations, he classified as a "far milder form of warfare." Civil strife (of which the character Theognis speaks in the *Laws*) is a far higher test of loyalty and of man's character than foreign wars. He who is loyal in "civil broil is worth his weight in gold and silver," since he is showing all the virtues: justice, temperance, and wisdom, as well as courage. In civil strife the greatest virtue is "loyalty in the hour of danger," which "may be truly called perfect justice." Foreign wars (of which the character Tyrtacus speaks) are often fought by mercenaries who "are generally and without exception insolent, unjust, violent men, and the most sinister of human beings." Their courage ranks as a "fourth-rate" virtue after justice, temperance, and wisdom. (*Laws I*, p. 412.)

Aristotle in Book VIII of his *Nichomachean Ethics* deals with the quality called *philia* (often translated as "friendship," "harmony," or "good will"), the bond that holds the members of any association together, the bond that gives different people something in common, regardless of whether the association is a city-state, family, or business association. Aristotle's views are therefore most germane to the question of loyalty, and the term "loyalty" here, for the purpose of our discussion, may be used interchangeably with *philia*. There are three motives, according to Aristotle, that are the basis of loyalty (or friendship): usefulness, time for pleasure, and the basis of virtue or excellence. *(Nicomachean Ethics*, trans. by Martin Ostwald, Bobbs-Merrill, 1962, pp. 218 – 226.)

When loyalty is based only on usefulness, people "do not find joy in one another, unless they see some material advantage coming to them." The same is true of loyalty based on pleasure. Loyalty that owes its existence to these two motives disappears with the disappearance of the motives. In our time, the "loyalty" of gangsters to their boss and loyalty to tyrants or corrupted politicians will fall under this classification. When the leader of a major underworld criminal "family" is assassinated, its members will pledge loyalty to the new chief of mobsters. When a tyrant is overthrown, his palace guard or secret police will offer its services to the new dictator who spearheaded the rebellion and moved into the presidential palace. The loyalty of those who base it on utility or on pleasure dissolves as soon "as it ceases to be to their advantage, since they were friends not of one another but [of] what was profitable for them."

The perfect form of loyalty is "when people are friends on the basis of virtue or excellence." This kind of loyalty implies mutual trust and has the characteristic of being lasting. It consists in giving rather than in receiving affection. It tends to be unique, because it is impossible to extend perfect loyalty to many people or causes, just as it is impossible, stated Aristotle, "to be in love with many people at the same time. For love is like an extreme, and an extreme tends to be unique."

In their demand for loyalty to the city-state, Plato and Aristotle make a distinction between "true" and corrupt governments. The three forms of government are kingship, aristocracy, and democracy. (Aristotle uses the term "timocracy"—government of property owners—in place of "democracy.") Of the three, states Aristotle, kingship is the best, provided that the king acts as a "shepherd of the people," looking out for his subjects. The king turns into a tyrant when he violates the laws and pursues his own good. In tyranny there is little or no place for loyalty (friendship). There is also no place for loyalty when aristocracy changes into oligarchy and the wicked rulers "take all or most things for themselves." (*Nicomachean Ethics*, p. 234).

For Plato it is possible to bisect all governments according to whether they do or do not adhere to the principles of law. Democracy may rule with law or without law. Monarchy is "divided into royalty and tyranny," and the rule of few is divided into aristocracy and oligarchy. (*The Statesman*, *The Dialogues of Plato*, p. 330.) Although democracy, according to Aristotle, is the worst of the three forms of government, he admits that of the perverted forms of government "democracy is the least wicked," since "where the citizens are equal, they have many things in common." (*Nicomachean Ethics*, pp. 236 – 237.)

Loyalty is not expressly mentioned by Aristotle, but it is clearly implied as a virtue of a good man whose noble actions are of benefit to his fellowman. He describes the actions that give nobility to a virtuous man's conduct as follows:

"It is also true that many actions of a man of high moral standards are performed in the interest of his friends and of his country. And if there be need, he will give his life for them. He will freely give his money, hours, and, in short, all goods, things that men compete for, while he gains nobility for himself. . . . No wonder, then, that he is regarded as a man of high moral standards, since he chooses nobility at the cost of everything else. . . ." (*Ibid.*, Book IX, pp. 262 – 263).

Aristotle in his treatise on *Politics* expects from the rulers, in addition to their capacity to govern, loyalty to the "State or political association" and virtue and justice compatible with the polity. In his discussion of how the well-being of the polity may best be served, he recommends education in the spirit of the polity: "Without this education the wisest laws are futile."

Plato and Aristotle in their discussion of love and devotion to the city do not bring up the problem of conflicting loyalties, for example, the conflict between loyalty to the state and personal loyalty to family members or friends. In Sophocles' *Antigone*, the classic tragedy of the remnants of the house of Oedipus, Creon, upon assuming political power in the aftermath of civil war, is faced with Antigone's act of disobedience. In the passionate debate in which Sophocles explores the issues of political expediency and conscientious objection, there is no explicit reference to loyalty, but the dilemma Antigone faces directly pertains to the conflict of loyalties. She disobeys the existing law (that no one is to bury the body of her dead brother Polyneices, since he led a war against the state) because of her two loyalties: first, her loyalty to the laws of the gods and "the lawful traditions that the gods have not written merely, but made infallible," which she does not intend to break because of "fear of one man and his principles"; and, second, her own sense of personal loyalty, which prompts her to say that "if I had let my own brother stay unburied I would have suffered all the pain I do not feel now."

Cicero undertook an analysis of conflicting loyalties to the city-state and to a friend in his *De Amicitia*. To answer the question of how far a loyalty to a friend ought to go when it conflicts with loyalty to the state, Cicero elaborates movingly on the concept of friendship. He recognizes friendship as one of the infinite ties uniting the human race and "fashioned by Nature itself." He urges people, therefore, to put friendship above all human things, for nothing is more in harmony with nature than friendship and "nothing so adaptable to our fortunes whether they be favourable or adverse." (Trans. by William Armstead Falconer, Harvard University Press, 1971, p. 127.)

Since friendship emanates directly from nature rather than from need, it must be genuine and come "of its own accord," with a feeling of love, rather than from calculation of how much profit the friendship is likely to afford. In order to obtain some advantages under the pretense of friendship, some are courted and honored "to suit the occasion; yet in true friendship there is nothing false, nothing pretended." (*Ibid.*, p. 139.)

Friendship, according to Cicero, exists only among "good men." Who are they? They are those "who so act and so live as to give proof of loyalty and uprightness, of fairness and generosity; who are free from all passion, caprice, and insolence, and have great strength of character. . . ." One of the qualities of friendship is unswerving constancy, which is obtained only through loyalty, "for nothing is constant that is disloyal. . . ." *(Ibid.*, p. 175.) What are the laws of friendship concerning the limits of loyalty when demands are made that one should do something that is wrong and dishonorable? Are, for instance, friends bound for the sake of friendship when asked to bear arms against their country?

In *De Amicitia,* this question arose in Cicero's conversation with Gaius Blossius Cumae, who came to him to plead for leniency for his support of Tiberius Gracchus, offering as a reason for a pardon that in his loyalty to Tiberius Gracchus it was his duty to do anything that Tiberius requested him. (Tiberius was a tribune and avowed reformer who passed the agrarian laws to redistribute the public land which the rich had taken over. When at election time he renominated himself, the senate declared it illegal and the election was postponed. In a riot on the following day, Tiberius was murdered.) Asked Cicero: "Even if he requested you to set fire to the Capitol?" Responded Gaius, ". . . [I]f he had I should have obeyed." *(Ibid.,* p. 149.)

Cicero found this attitude of Gaius' an ungodly one. Loyalty cannot go so far as to cause a person to commit a crime against the Republic. The first law of friendship is to do for friends only what is honorable. This law forbids one to ask a friend to perform dishonorable acts or to do them himself if asked. There is no justification to sin on behalf of a friend. In case of a conflict of loyalties, it is dishonorable for anyone to

plead loyalty to a friend in defense of sin in general
and especially of those sins against the state committed for "the sake of a friend." No one, according to
Cicero, can argue that it is permissible to follow a
friend "when waging war against his country." (*Ibid.*,
pp. 151 – 158.)

It may be pointed out that Cicero's position was not
always shared by other philosophers and writers. In
the Middle Ages, Dante (1265 – 1321), the outstanding Italian poet and one of the great figures of world
literature, in his *Divine Comedy* placed Brutus and
Cassius in the lowest circle of Hell because they had
chosen to betray their friend Julius Caesar rather than
their country, Rome. In modern times the English
novelist E. M. Forster in *Two Cheers for Democracy*
deplores the fact that in our generation personal
relations are "despised" and replaced by a trend to
dedicate ourselves to some movement or cause. "I
hate the idea of causes," wrote Forster, "and if I had
to choose between betraying my country and betraying my friend, I hope I should have the guts to betray
my country." (Harcourt, Brace and Company, 1951,
p. 68.) I shall return to the issue of conflicting loyalties in my discussion of just purpose.

Feudal Loyalty

In the ancient writing I have been examining,
loyalty finds its expression in discussions of friendship, *philia,* and love of one's country. In the Middle
Ages, the basic social structure of Western Europe
became the local agricultural and political economy.
With this new structure came new concepts of loyalty.

With the dissolution of Charlemagne's empire and the breakdown of central government, people turned to the powerful landowners for protection. The alliance of the protector—the noble landowner—and of his subordinates grew into the feudal system. The foundation of this feudal relationship was the *fief* (which gave feudalism its name), which was usually land. The grantor of the fief was the lord, and the recipient was the vassal.

The lord granted the vassal protection and the use of land in return for personal services and duties. To acquire his fief, the vassal knelt before the lord, put his hands between the lord's hands, and swore an oath to be loyal to the lord and to perform the services and acts due to him. This was an act of homage or an act of fealty. The overlord bound himself by kissing the vassal and lifting him to his feet. By an act of investiture, he invested the vassal with the possession of the fief. The investiture called for giving to the vassal a symbol of land transferred (a straw, a clod of earth, or a stick).

There was a hierarchy of lords (knights, counts, dukes, barons, earls, and other nobles) with a series of loyalties that progressed upward from the vassal to the supreme overlord, the king. For the protection provided by the lord, the vassal had an obligation to supply a stipulated number of armed men, in addition to dues and services varying with local customs. The concentration of power into single hands by the rise of monarchies in Europe and the expansion of the economic world after the crusades broke down the feudal system by the end of the fourteenth century.

The ceremony of homage and investiture con-

stituted a contract that hardly included the concept of
personal loyalty (a distinction should be made here
between loyalty and fealty). No personal attachment
existed between the vassal and his lord that
commanded a free, devoted service to him or to a
certain cause. Fealty commanded only the respect of
faith to the pledge made by the vassal in the act of
homage to his overlord. Since it was not backed by
sentiments of personal allegiance, the contract of
feudalism offered loyalty to an office, rather than to a
person. Loyalty to the office of the king did permit
resistance to an evil tyrant.

The Magna Charta—which King John was forced to
agree to because of a revolt of the barons in 1215—is
the most memorable document in English constitutional history. The "Great Charter," called the
"palladium of English liberty," gave the barons
guarantees against oppression and abuse of the king's
prerogatives. The barons exacted from King John the
commitment that he would not encroach on their own
rights and privileges. The Charter became a symbol of
the supremacy of the law of the land over the king. Its
thirty-ninth clause provides that no free man may be
"imprisoned, outlawed, exiled, condemned, or in any
way destroyed" unless according to the law of the
land.

The importance of the concessions of the Magna
Charta that were wrung from the king is that they set
forth a distinction between loyalty to the office and
loyalty to the man in the office. England became a
legal, not a regal, state. The Charter put limitations
upon the power of the king, and thus violation of any
of the articles of the Charter justified a rebellion

against the king. Loyalty to the office of the king did not call for loyalty to a king who transgressed his legal powers.

Loyalty to God and Loyalty to the Church

King John was opposed not only by the barons but also by churchmen headed by Stephen Langton. The church participated in and influenced the feudal system, and some aspects of its hierarchy paralleled the feudal hierarchy. But the position of the church in society was complicated by another important concept of loyalty; in this concept, the most important loyalty was not to another individual, to a ruler, or even to the state, but to God.

A. The Hebrew Tradition

To the ancient Hebrews, the idea of loyalty was distinctly religious. They tried to please God and shrank from arousing His anger. The first four Commandments sum up duties of men toward God, and they clearly took precedence over the remaining Commandments, which summarize the duties of men toward each other. Obedience to all of them is regarded as a duty to God, the holy lawgiver. Any act of disloyalty was, therefore, sinful. Psalm 119 is an expression of the Psalmist's spirit of loyalty in his desire to fulfill the Divine Law to its end. In his inward obedience to the law of his God, he prays, "Give me understanding and I shall keep the law; Yea, I shall observe it with all my heart." He prays for help in obeying and in applying the divine law and for help in

putting himself in accordance with the spirit
established by God's word.

The Old and the New Testaments make a distinction between legalism and loyalty. The legalist
performs his duty by not breaking the rules. The
loyalist, upheld by his faith, puts his whole heart into
his duty and sets no limits for fulfillment of the law. "A
good man out of the good treasure of his heart
bringeth that which is good." (Luke 6:45.) Israel as a
whole was regarded as God's "firstborn son" (Exodus
4:22), and a man was only a fractional part of a chosen
nation. When Achan sinned against God, he and his
family were stoned and all their possessions burned to
turn the Lord from "the fierceness of his anger"
against Israel. (Joshua 7:25 – 26.)

The Covenant relation of Israel as a nation to
Jehovah was the standard by which loyalty to God was
to be judged. The nation's deference to the Covenant
meant loyalty to God. (Hosea 6:7; Amos 3:1 – 3.)
Although in the teachings of Jeremiah and Ezekiel,
individual responsibility is singled out ("Every one
shall die for his own iniquity," Jeremiah 31:30;
Ezekiel 18:2 – 4), the prophets never abandoned the
idea that national well-being depended upon walking
"humbly with God." (Micah 6:8.)

The classical example of loyalty is the tragic offering
of Isaac on the mountain of Moriah. Archeological discoveries, such as skeletons of young infants, give
evidence that among the Canaanites there was a
widespread custom of sacrificing the firstborn (like the
first fruits or the first harvest) as sacred to divinity.
Abraham, to provide his loyalty to God, sought to act
according to the existing, perverted standards. Be-

cause of Abraham's readiness to sacrifice his only son, his loyalty was rewarded by the Lord's blessing. (Genesis 22:17.) Similarly, the unfailing loyalty of Jonathan, the son of Saul, to David is marked with a genuineness displayed by his efforts to save David from Saul's jealousy. The gratitude of David for Jonathan's loyalty and friendship is expressed in his eulogy on the occasion of Jonathan's death. (II Samuel 1:17 – 27.)

The idea of loyalty to God reaches a climax in the Book of Job. In this book a sage who has always done what the Lord required of him is afflicted with an incurable, painful malady. Because he has been afflicted with a loathsome disease, his friends abandon him and question his integrity. Yet, in all his suffering, Job holds up the lofty idea of loyalty to God's love and mercy. God's plan to discipline his followers includes suffering, which may be for the welfare of others. (Job 22:30.) This kind of allegiance to the Lord's laws and attachment to His authority in time of suffering kept the Jews together in exile.

B. *The Christian Tradition*

In the New Testament, communion with God can be effected only through Christ. The priesthood of Jesus removed all barriers between men and God, and loyalty to God rests on three virtues that converge in Christ: faith, hope, and love. The Mosaic law based loyalty to God on the penalty of punishment if the law is not obeyed. Jesus taught that such loyalty to God should be rendered out of love of Him and of His righteousness. Loyalty should emanate from integrity of heart and the demands of God and should be distinguished from ceremonial obligation: "Nothing that goes into a man from outside can defile him; no, it is the things that come out of him that defile a man." (Mark 7:15.) Forbearance and renunciation must be cultivated in order for a person to enter the spiritual kingdom of heaven.

After the ascendancy of Christianity to a position of worldly power during the time of Constantine, the issue of loyalty to God became entangled with the problems of loyalty to the church as an institution with influence in the world. St. Augustine (354 – 430)—the founder of theology, whose influence on Christianity is thought by many to be second only to that of St. Paul—had a great impact on the Middle Ages with his idea of the validity of worldly rule by the church. In *The City of God*, he foresaw the rising of Christianity into an empire on the ruins of Rome. He projected the role of the church as the divine-led ruler over all nations bound by common loyalty to the church.

In this earthly world, Augustine took the position that there is a duty of loyalty to an evil, as well as to a righteous, ruler since "God gives happiness in the kingdom of heaven to the pious alone, but gives kingly power on earth both to the pious and the impious, as it may please Him. . . ." Even the dreaded Nero Caesar, who reached, according to Augustine, the summit of vice and cruelty, ruled by the will of God because "power and domination are not given even to such men save by the providence of the most high

God, when he judges that the state of human affairs is worthy of such lords." Tyrants rule as a punishment for sins, and we fulfill God's purpose through loyalty to Him, because behind each act of God there is a "hidden cause, known better to God than to us, depending on the diversity of the merits of the human race." (*St. Augustine's City of God, A Select Library of the Nicene and Post Nicene Fathers of the Christian Church,* Vol. II, ed. Philip Schaff, Wm. Eerdmans, 1979, pp. 101 – 103.)

The idea of the unity of Christendom and the idea that the world should be turned into an organized Kingdom of Heaven where the underpinnings of the theory that the kings of terrestrial states owe loyalty to the Pope, the high priest and the divine monarch of Christendom. This idea of a divine world dominion ruled by the church, which would bring about the peace of Christ thoughout the world, was nourished by the church throughout the Middle Ages. This idea, however, did not appeal to the secular world, and from the fifth through the fifteenth centuries, history records a divergence of views about the role of the church and the consequent failure of the idea of a divine world government.

C. St. Thomas Aquinas

Another principal saint and doctor of the Roman Catholic Church, St. Thomas Aquinas (1225 – 1274), differs from Augustine by declaring the right to resist tyranny. His monumental contention was that reason and faith cannot deny each other's findings, although they may differ in their procedure. (This idea was opposed to another strand of thought arising in the thirteenth century, represented by the Arab philosopher Averroes and the Franciscan scholastic philosophers Duns Scotus and William of Occam, that truth in faith need not be compatible with reason and that there cannot be a rational demonstration of God's existence and of the immortality of the soul.) Aquinas in the *Summa Theologica* reaches the conclusion—based both on reason and on faith—that "Man is bound to obey secular princes in so far as this is required by the order of justice. Wherefore if the prince's authority is not just but usurped, or if he commands what is unjust, his subjects are not bound to obey him." Aquinas sees no sedition in being disloyal to a tyrant because "indeed it is the tyrant rather that is guilty of sedition since he encourages discord and sedition among his subjects, that he may lord over them more securely; for this is tyranny, being conducive to the private good of the ruler, and to the injury of the multitude."

St. Thomas makes the distinction between loyalty to the office and loyalty to the tyrant occupying the office. He advocates obedience as a "special virtue," but in matters concerning human behavior, "a subject is bound to obey his superior only within the sphere of his authority." Aquinas also makes a clear distinction between the subject's loyalty to God and to his earthly superior. There are some matters in which no earthly master has jurisdiction and in which one owes obedience only to God. Only in matters where the "superior stands between God and his subjects" is the subject bound to obey his superior, whereas "in respect of other matters the subject is immediately under God, by Whom he is taught either by the natural or by written law." (*Summa Theologica*, Vol. III, Christian Classics, 1948.)

The Renaissance—The Divorce of Loyalty from Ethics

The period of transition from medieval to modern times known as the Renaissance, which is generally identified as stretching from the fourteenth through the seventeenth century, is marked by a flowering of creative literature, by the rebirth of classic architecture and the development of cities with distinctive and beautiful buildings, by economic changes brought by the Crusades that had opened the routes to the East, by discoveries and inventions that tended to civilize the life of man, and by the patronage of artists by princes and men of wealth. It was an age of social and intellectual achievement in the field of science, in the exploration of the world, and in the conquest of the seas and of man's ignorance about the mysteries of the sky and the earth. In this age of change, Columbus landed on the shores of the New World, and Europe started to reap the benefits to be derived from the discovery of America.

A. *Machiavelli*

The Renaissance was the age of a weakening of the hold of the Catholic Church upon the consciences of men and of the concentration of power in the hands of European monarchs, such as the Holy Roman Emperor Charles V (who held sway over more territory than any other European ruler), King Francis I of France, and King Henry VIII of England. The art of kingcraft suitable for such monarchs was expounded by such political theorists as Niccolo Machiavelli (1469 – 1527) and Thomas Hobbes (1588 – 1679). Their powerful minds spread their influence everywhere, and their ideas were received as the quintessence of political wisdom. By divorcing the study of politics from the study of ethics, Machiavelli and Hobbes completely dissevered themselves from the older concepts of the power of conscience in men, as well as from traditional concepts of loyalty.

Machiavelli saw as the core of political success and effectiveness force unrestricted by considerations of generally accepted moral values. In order to achieve political ends, he argued, a ruler may lie, deceive, intrigue, conspire, or use any kind of crooked means. The ruler "must not mind incurring the charge of cruelty for the purpose of keeping the subjects united and faithful." (*The Prince*, The New Library, 1952, p. 89.) The Duke of Gloucester (later Richard III) in Shakespeare's *Henry VI* personifies Machiavelli's ideas calling for complete disregard of moral bonds and responsibilities when he declares:

> "Why, I can smile, and murder whiles I smile;
> And cry content to that which grieves my heart;
> And wet my cheeks with artificial tears,
> And frame my face to all occasions. . . .
> I can add colours to the chameleon;
> Change shapes with Proteus for advantages;
> And set the murderous Machiavel to school.
> Can I do this, and cannot get a crown?"

Born in 1469, Machiavelli witnessed the troubled political life of his native Florence and concluded that the only way for the state to become a dynamic, aggressive entity was to increase the power of the prince. In foreign policy, the prince should seek to defend his less powerful neighbors and to weaken the stronger ones. "A prince should therefore have no other aim or thought, nor take up any other thing for his study, but war and its organization and discipline, for that is the only art that is necessary to one who commands. . . ." (*Ibid.*, pp. 46–47.) (It seems that *The Prince* continues to serve as a handbook for Soviet rulers in their policy toward the satellites in Eastern Europe and toward minorities at home.)

On the domestic front, Machiavelli argued, the policies of the prince should also be divorced from moral values. Since it is difficult for a ruler to be both loved and feared, "it is much safer to be feared than loved." (*Ibid.*, p. 90.) Although it seems advisable for the prince to be merciful, faithful, humane, sincere, and religious, "in order to maintain the state" he should not hesitate "to act against faith, against charity, against humanity, and against religion." (*Ibid.*, p. 93.) Machiavelli suggests that the prince discourage attempts to advise him (unless he asks for such advice), "for men will always be false to you unless they are compelled by necessity to be true." (*Ibid.*, p. 117.) The prince should use hypocrisy, since it is expedient for him to seem to his subjects "all mercy, faith, integrity, humanity and religion." (*Ibid.*, p. 94.)

If, according to Machiavelli, the prince should violate any kind of legal and moral commitments in the interest of self-aggrandisement and absolute power, the question arises, what are the responsibilities of his subjects when the prince abuses his powers? Is there a place for loyalty to the prince who is outside law, integrity, and morality? Although it seems that any kind of evil is condoned within the precepts of Machiavellianism, a closer examination of Machiavelli's writings will reveal his awareness of the importance of traditional moral values, such as loyalty, patriotism, and love. He was keenly aware of the importance of loyalty when he recommended that the prince should have the loyalty of the people, because force is not enough and "it is necessary for a prince to possess the friendship of the people; otherwise he has no resource in times of adversity." *(Ibid.,* p. 65.)

Machiavelli in the *Discourses* also acknowledges that the power of the state must be endowed with lawful authority in order for it to endure. He asked the reader to note

> "how much more praise those Emperors merited who, after Rome became an empire, conformed to the laws like good princes, than those who took the opposite course; and he will see that Titus, Nerva, Trajan, Hadrian, Antoninus, and Marcus Aurelius did not require the Praetorians nor the multitudinous legions to defend them, because they were protected by their own good conduct, [by] the good will of the people, and by the love of the Senate."

Machiavelli's passionate love for Italy and his recognition of the importance of such virtues as loyalty, mercy, faith, and integrity show that some historians—in spite of the identification of his precepts with everything that is considered to be immoral and inhuman—are justified in hailing him as a leading political philosopher and the founder of modern political science.

B. Hobbes

The whole tenor of Machiavelli's thought about the omnipotent prince was echoed by the English philosopher who exalted absolute monarchy, Thomas Hobbes. The foundation of his ethics is the doctrine of the original nature of man. According to the fundamental law of nature, every man has the right to everything, and when he cannot obtain all that he desires, he "may seek, and use, all helps, and advantages of war." From this law derives the second law, that a man is willing, when others are also, to lay down his selfish rights to create the state, "and he contended with so much liberty against other men, as he would allow other men against himself." (*Leviathan*, Basil Blackwell, 1960, p. 85.)

This surrender of rights and establishment of an absolute sovereignty, Hobbes contends, is a contract made by "every man with every man." This agreement is made by people with each other, not with the sovereign. To obtain peace and secure the common defense, men "confer all their power and strength upon one man, or upon an assembly of men," and by doing so "they may reduce all their wills, by plurality of voices unto one will." In other words, the covenant is made in such a manner as if every man would say to every other man, "I authorize and give up my right of governing myself, to this man, or to this assembly of men, on this condition, that you give up thy right to him, and authorize all his actions in like manner." (*Ibid.*, p. 12.)

In a civil society that is the creation of a covenant between men, peace and security are obtained at the price of replacing freedom by law and rights by obligation. By the voluntary surrender of the natural right of each man to an authority, a new entity, which Hobbes calls an "artificial man," is created, a commonwealth. There are, according to Hobbes, three types of commonwealth—monarchy, aristocracy, and democracy. The sovereignty residing in monarchy is absolutely supreme and outside the restraints of the contract: "There can happen no breach of covenant on the part of the sovereign; and consequently none of his subjects, by any pretense of forfeiture, can be freed from his subjection." (*Ibid.*, p. 114.)

Hobbes makes no distinction between a good and a tyrannical government, "because the name of tyranny signifieth nothing more, nor less than the name of sovereignty, be it in one, or many men, saving that they that use the former word, are understood to be angry with them they call tyrants." (*Ibid.*, p. 463.) Supreme power is indispensable for supreme authority, and only power can perpetually enforce the covenant made by people with each other: "Covenants without the Sword, are but words." Without force and terror the laws of a higher nature, such as justice, modesty, and mercy, could not be enforced since they are contrary to man's natural passions of "pride, revenge, and the like." (*Ibid.*, p. 109.)

Is there a place for loyalty in "this great Leviathan, which is called the State"? Hardly, since loyalty is replaced by total submission of the subject to the ruler. To ensure the order of the commonwealth, there must be obedience to the will of the sovereign. This idea also implies a lack of loyalty to one's country. If a subject becomes a prisoner in war and can save his life by becoming subject to the victor, "he hath the liberty to accept the condition, and having accepted it, is the subject of him that took him." Furthermore, if the monarch subdued by war renders himself to become a subject of the victor, his subjects "become obliged to the victor." (*Ibid.*, p. 145.) There is no personal loyalty to the monarch; whoever conquers and provides security and peace ought to be obeyed.

The Dominant Role of the People

It is not surprising that the immoral tendencies of Hobbes' doctrines aroused a storm of abuse as well as serious criticism. He was denounced for being an apostle of despotism, for holding religion in contempt, and for teaching, as one of his critics expressed it, "one of the meanest of all ethical theories." The most important antagonists of Hobbes' concept of a contract of submission were John Locke, who assigned in the contractual relation a dominant role to the people and a subservient role to the government, and Jean-Jacques Rousseau, who completely rejected the concept of the contract of government.

A. *John Locke*

John Locke (1632 – 1704), called the "founder of British empiricism," saw the justification of government in the consent of the governed, based on the natural rights of the people. He differentiated the origins of a society from the establishment of the government. Refuting the Hobbesian thesis of the anarchistic and savage state of nature before the establishment of government, Locke maintained that men in the state of nature were free, equal, and independent and that no one could be "put out of this estate and subjected to the political power of another without his own consent." (*Two Treatises of Government*, ed. Thomas T. Cook, Hofner Publishing Company, 1947, p. 168.) The law of the state of nature is reason, which commands that no one should injure another's freedom, life, or property. In remitting power to the majority, men enter society by their own consent. The law established by a majority vote is the only effective method of arriving at decisions in a society aimed at common good.

In support of his theory that the governments of the world were begun in peace and by the consent of the people, Locke lists examples of history. One place he found evidence was in the writings of Jose de Orcosta, a Spanish Jesuit and a missionary to Peru, who in his *Historia Natural y Moral de las Indias* reported that many parts of America had neither kings nor commonwealth, but as the occasion demanded it, they chose their "captains as they please." Locke also frequently quoted the history of Israel. An example is his reference to the passage in the Book of Judges where the Gileadites ask Jephthah to assist them against the Ammonites, "and the people made him head and captain over them." (Judges 11:2.)

The actual use of an agreement between individuals to compose a society is found in the declaration made by the Pilgrim Fathers on the *Mayflower* in 1620, in which occurs the phrase, "We do solemnly and mutually, in the presence of God and of one another, covenant and combine ourselves together into a civil body politic." The natural implication of such an agreement is that the government, as a servant of society, is bound by the provisions by which it had been established and by the will of a free people.

Although the state of nature was governed by law, according to Locke, disputes arose among men engaged in the pursuit of their individual rights. The purpose of political society was to overcome the lack of an authority to judge the controversies between the parties engaged in disputes. The state thus became a judicial body interpreting the law of nature for individuals. This does not mean at all that the state can deprive these individuals of their natural rights. Through the social contract, the individual preserves his natural rights, giving up only the part necessary for the community to live effectively. This arrangement between people and their rulers differentiates the loyalty of the people from the loyalty of the rulers.

The loyalty of individuals consists of reverence for law and respect for authority. Since the people are dominant and the government is subservient, the loyalty of a ruler consists not only in adhering to the laws that bind his power but also in making the well-being of the public the end purpose of his government. Consequently, whosoever in authority exceeds the power given him by the law and makes improper use of the force he has under his command, "may be opposed as any other man who by force invades the right of another." (*Two Treatises of Government*, p. 224.)

People owe no loyalty to those who commit a breach of trust, subvert the government, and poison "the fountain of public security." Locke—who witnessed the civil war and the "Glorious Revolution" (which deposed King James II, according to the resolution passed by the 1688 Convention parliament)—justifies the revolt of the British people against tyranny, thus setting a precedent for the justification of the American Revolution. According to a similar argument, the contract by which the American colonists promised allegiance to the British crown was broken by George III. It was their right to resist his illegal use of authority and to redirect political power into avenues reflecting the will of the people.

B. Common Loyalty to a Just Purpose

Locke's concept of a society based on a "compact" (which we would call a "constitution"), which covers the terms of the people's agreement to form a society, and on "trust," the fiduciary relation that determines the limits of the government's power, was adopted by Thomas Paine, the brilliant Englishman whose pamphlet entitled *Common Sense* had an enormous effect on American colonists. His appeal, "The blood of the slain, the weeping voice of nature cries, 'Tis time to part,' " convinced thousands of colonists of the necessity to separate from England. In his *The Rights of Man*, Thomas Paine assigned to the people the role of a superior partner in their relations with the government. The people have natural rights, according to Paine, while the government has mainly an obligation to be the servant of society.

The impact of the powerful teaching of Locke on the framers of our Constitution is not limited to the justification of the right of resistance to unjust and unlawful force. His concept of natural rights became a universal claim of mankind. Declarations marked by ideas of natural rights guaranteeing that citizens would not be abused by the government preface the Declaration of Independence and the constitutions adopted between 1776 and 1783 by Maryland, Massachusetts, New Hampshire, South Carolina, Vermont, and Virginia. The universalism of the natural law idea also marks the French Declaration of the Rights of Man and of the Citizen (1789), which proclaimed that the purpose of every political association is "the preservation of the natural and imprescriptible rights of man," which include the right to resist oppression.

It should be noted that our Declaration of Independence with its indictment of the King of England did not see in the rights of Americans as a nationality the reason for forming a new state. Rather, it justified the founding of our nation on the need to protect the fundamental human rights to life, liberty, and the pursuit of happiness that had been violated by

the king. The United States was unique, at the time of
its founding, in that its cohesiveness was based not
simply on geographical, racial, or linguistic ties but
rather on an allegiance to the conception of natural
rights which are beyond the reach of any government
and which transcend geographical boundaries.

The Constitution should always be read in the spirit
of this loyalty, which is not to a king or to a piece of
territory but to a purpose, namely that of protecting
citizens against the exercise of arbitrary and capri-
cious power by the government. As an outstanding ex-
ponent of the political philosophy of American
history, Hans J. Morgenthau, expressed it:

> "A nation which was built upon a common loyalty
> to a certain purpose, whose citizens have come
> together voluntarily to share in the achievement
> of that purpose, which owes its very existence to
> a revolt against arbitrary impediments to the
> achievement of that purpose—such a nation stands
> or falls, as a nation, with its loyalty to that
> purpose." (*The Purpose of American Politics*,
> Vintage Books, 1960, p. 56.)

In support of the "self-evident truth" that all men
are endowed with certain unalienable rights, that the
governments derive their just powers from the consent of the governed, and that it is the right of the
people to abolish a government that "becomes
destructive of these ends," the representatives of the
twelve states that agreed to the text of the Declaration
pledged to each other "our lives, our fortunes and our
sacred honor." They found a goal, an "American
purpose" to which they pledged their common loyalty

"with a firm reliance on the protection of divine Providence."

The Constitution and the American political system are the living manifestation of the silent compact between citizens and their government to cooperate in the achievement of this purpose. Such a purpose—to which we are referring in our definition of loyalty as a "just purpose"—makes moral demands on our attitudes and actions. These demands have been met in some of our national achievements, but they have also been answered with denials and by sporadic violations of that purpose. The failures can be explained by the fact that, in the search for the substance of the "common" and "just" purpose we seek, we are confronted with a conflict of views, some of them too narrow and others too exhaustive. These diverse views range from single-minded, exclusive loyalty to a leader or movement to a pluralistic loyalty resulting from the interaction of coexisting and competing loyalties to religious, economic, natural, or racial groups.

Multiple and Competing Loyalties

Single loyalty provides no safer path to the achievement of the purpose of equality in freedom through a common loyalty (the ideal to which our forefathers pledged themselves) than pluralistic loyalty does. History gives us numerous examples of followers of a leader or of a movement who have been browbeaten into rejecting their religious and political beliefs and their families and into betraying their friends in order to make them utterly devoted to their leader and his movement. Hitler demanded and received absolute loyalty, and Khoumeni is regarded as a fountain of wisdom by his followers.

In the case of multiple loyalties, the common loyalty is endangered when one of the competing loyalties is raised above this loyalty to the "certain purpose" which the founders of this country agreed to achieve. This purpose can be achieved only when the spirit of reconciliation, not of hate, is at the heart of the multiple loyalties to labor unions, industrial organizations, and national, racial, or religious groups. This purpose can be achieved when behind each loyalty lies an understanding of the law of sowing and reaping, when a law of service and sacrifice underlies its existence.

Some denials of the American purpose should be attributed to the fact that a distinction should be drawn between the moral and social behavior of individuals and of racial, national, and economic groups. Human societies and social groups have less capacity than individual men and women to comprehend the needs of others and less ability to consider interests other than their own. As Reinhold Niebuhr pointed out, a human group has less ability to comprehend the needs of others and more unrestrained egoism than the individuals who compose the group. Individuals are capable, on occasion, of preferring the advantages of others to their own, and their sentiments of sympathy and sense of justice can lead them in the direction of altruism. The morality of groups is, however, inferior to that of individuals.

Man's collective behavior, because of collective egoism, "can never be brought completely under the dominion of reason or conscience." *(Moral Man and Immoral Society,* Charles Scribner's Sons, 1960, p. xii.) The truths proclaimed as "self-evident" by our forefathers appeared meaningless and not "self-evident" at all to some of the political groups that shaped the history of our nation.

One example of the discrepancy between private and public morality looms large in the history of our country. In the worlds of Lincoln, the Declaration of Independence "gave promise that in due time the weights should be lifted from the shoulders of all men" in the world. Jefferson warned that our "falling into anarchy would decide forever the destinies of mankind, and seal the political heresy that man is incapable of self-government" since we are "the only depositories of the sacred fire of liberty." And, yet, the framers of the Constitution compromised the principle of equality—which had been enshrined so nobly in the Declaration of Independence in the famous phrase "all men are created equal"—with its antithesis, slavery.

Multiple loyalties can create tensions, but competing loyalties should not debilitate the spirit of common purpose that should characterize our nation, since the denial of this purpose will alienate the people from America itself. The thoughts of the French statesman Turgot, expressed in a letter of March 22, 1778, concerning Americans and their new republican government, reflect the sentiment shared today by oppressed countries:

"They are the hope of the human race. They should be the model. They must prove to the world, as a fact, that men can be both free and peaceful and can dispense with the trammels of all sorts which tyrants and charlatans of every costume have presumed to impose under the pretext of public safety. They must give the example of political liberty, of religious liberty, of commercial and industrial liberty. The asylum which America affords to the oppressed of all nations will console the world."

A common loyalty faces the danger of failure to obtain a general consensus because we try to find legitimacy in pluralistic loyalties to all aspects of society's life, including our relations to the church, to the state, and to various economic, political, racial, and national groups. Among the tensions caused by multiple loyalties, the freedoms of religion, of speech, and of association have been at the heart of the so-called loyalty controversies that have occurred throughout our history. Broadly speaking, common loyalty to the American purpose embodies a standard of devotion to our country that satisfies a sense of fairness and good citizenship. It is not imprisoned within the limits of any rigid formula or within a fixed content of the meaning of good citizenship. If common loyalty demands commitment to the well-being of our country, it should be expected that earnest citizens can hold contrary views and that such differences in opinion should in no way reflect on their common loyalty to the "American purpose." The discussion of some of these "loyalty controversies" may deepen our understanding of the meaning of common loyalty.

Conflicting Loyalties

A. *Church and State*

The history of the early Middle Ages is in large part the history of the struggle between the Popes in Rome and the emperors of Western Europe. The claims for power of the secular rulers were opposed by the Popes, who insisted upon their right to absolute rule of all Christendom and the supremacy of the church over emperors, kings, and princes. Papal Rome saw world dominion through the establishment of a religious government of mankind with its center in Rome as the only way to obtain the "peace of Christ throughout the world." These controversies between the secular rulers and Rome existed for centuries, whether in a suppressed state or in outward conflict.

The question of investiture, for instance—the argument whether the emperor or the Pope should appoint bishops—was one of the most serious controversies, since in many kingdoms the church had vast properties, levied taxes, and had its own law courts, with Rome serving as the highest court of appeals. Since the church had become a state within a state, with powers reaching far beyond spiritual functions, the matter of who had the decisive voice in appointing bishops who controlled large domains became a vital question.

Saint Augustine's idea of the world as a "spiritual society of the predestined faithful" developed into a political policy advocating the divinely led ruling power of the church over all nations. The City of God advocated by Augustine, however, was not satisfied with its role of enhancing the spiritual values preached by Jesus of Nazareth; it wanted to dominate the world.

B. The City of God and the City of Man

One purpose of the Crusades was to extend the influence of Rome, the Latin church, over the territories now known as the Middle East and to undermine the Eastern Empire with the emperor of Constantinople dominant in the Greek-speaking Orthodox church. One of the most important examples of outward, violent public conflict took place in the time of the Emperor Frederick II, who was twice excommunicated by Pope Gregory IX for failing to start on his promised crusade. Frederick II, in turn, denounced the corruption in the church and urged all the princes in Europe to confiscate church property.

When biblical beliefs flow into political life, the result is acknowledgment and respect for human rights, religious tolerance, and freedom of the individual conscience. The Reformation and the Enlightenment were revolts against theocratic, dogmatic ecclesiastical institutions and not against traditional biblical values. Martin Luther was a Catholic when he protested against ecclesiastical imperialism. The Protestants—using this term to apply to all those who dissented from the mother church—set themselves against complete allegiance to the priest, bishop, and Pope and not against allegiance to the Bible, which they accepted as the absolute norm and the sole arbitrator of religious doctrines. Opposition between the political and spiritual realms disappears when the two cities rest on a common foundation, the legacy of the Christian belief in the dignity and worth of every individual.

The religious influences on those who framed and adopted the Constitution cannot be denied. Among the framers of the Constitution were nineteen Episcopalians, eight Congregationalists, seven Presbyterians, two Roman Catholics, two Quakers, one Methodist, and one member of the Dutch Reformed Church. They represented a cross section of the American religious bodies of that day. Throughout the history of the United States there have always been reasonable accommodations between the church and state, such as tax exemptions for property used for religious purposes, tax deductibility of contributions to churches, and military chaplaincies.

The aggregate of the "self-evident truths" expressed in the Declaration of Independence and later in the Bill of Rights reflects the belief of the builders of the republic that only people with a moral purpose can be free and that freedom can survive if the people, beyond the purpose of mere survival, are governed by moral law, which has its roots in religion. The separation of church and state by the Founding Fathers of the Land of the Free did not imply that religion was considered merely as a private affair. On the contrary, religion has had a striking impact on the forming of our nation. In a nation "under God," which recognizes the dignity and worth of every human being, God is best honored by free men with liberty of conscience. In a free society, the government must, therefore, assert freedom of conscience as an in-

defeasible right of the individual, who is not accountable to the government or to others for his religious
beliefs.

The conviction, held by the great men who have
led our country, that freedom has its roots in a belief
in divine ordinance is demonstrated in many of the
most famous American documents. The writers of the
Declaration of Independence proclaimed the birth of
our nation "with a firm reliance on the protection of
Divine Providence." George Washington began his
inaugural address with "fervent supplication to that
Almighty Being who rules over the Universe" and in
his farewell address besought "the Almighty to avert
or mitigate" whatever evils the new republic might
face. Abraham Lincoln prayed at Gettysburg "that
this nation, under God, shall have a new birth of
freedom."

The religious atmosphere in this country, in the
words of Alexis de Tocqueville, "was the first thing
that struck him" on his arrival in the United States. In
his desire to understand the reason for this
phenomenon, he questioned "the faithful of all
communions." He particularly sought the society of
clergymen, who "are depositories of the various
creeds and have a personal interest in their survival."
His research convinced him that the "main reason for
the quiet sway of religion over their country was the
complete separation of church and state." "I have,"
he wrote, "no hesitation in stating that throughout my
stay in America I met nobody, lay or cleric, who did
not agree about that." (*Democracy in America*, trans.
by George Lawrence, Harper & Row Publishers,
1966, pp. 271–272.)

C. *Separation between Church and State*

Since religious and spiritual values are inter-connected with our political life, the questions arise: What is the meaning of the rule of law that builds "a wall of separation" between church and state? What is the relationship between our loyalties to the state and our loyalties to the church?

The first question on the constitutional guarantee of separation of church and state has been addressed extensively by the Supreme Court. The conclusions it has reached can be enumerated as follows:

> Neither state nor federal government can set up a church, nor make laws respecting an establishment of religion or prohibiting the free exercise thereof. Nor can any official, "high or petty," prescribe what shall be orthodox in religion or other matters of opinion or force citizens "to confer by word or act their faith therein."
>
> Neither state nor federal government can pass laws that aid one religion, aid all religions, or prefer one religion over another.
>
> Neither state nor federal government can, openly or secretly, participate in the affairs of any religious organizations or groups and vice versa.
>
> No tax in any amount, large or small, can be levied to support any religious activities or institutions, whatever they may be called or whatever form they may adopt to teach or practice religion.

Do these conclusions call for ignoring the traditional, biblical moral values in making political decisions? Not at all, unless we wish to eliminate the distinction between good and evil and convert our political system into a barbaric tyranny that robs individuals of their freedom and human rights. In making political decisions, we must, however, realize that in a world with tyrannical regimes armed with nuclear power it would be unfeasible to base political decisions solely on moral principles. As a matter of expediency and of mankind's survival, we must deal with totalitarian governments, but we should never disregard the reality of having nations enslaved in a large part of the world. In the international game of political power, the voices against the immorality of apartheid should be joined by voices against the atrocities committed by communist regimes. Under no circumstances should moral considerations be eliminated in assessing our political goals.

To answer the second question concerning our loyalties to the state and to the church, it should be noted that on the domestic scene some of the furor caused by the Supreme Court's interpretation of the rule of the separation of church and state has reached almost the stage of obsession. Permission for saying a school prayer, for instance, was attacked as vigorously as if granting that permission amounted to turning this country into a theocracy in Khoumeni's style. The so-called fundamentalists defend organized prayer during the school day with as much vigor as if allowing the prayer amounted to a remedy against the drug culture, the growth of crime, out-of-wedlock pregnancy, and the other highly disturbing trends in our society.

The interpretation that should be followed is sovereign reverence to the intentions of the framers of our Constitution, who did not expect the state to behave as if it were a church or the church to behave as if it were a state. James Madison, author of the First Amendment, wrote:

". . . [I]t is proper to take alarm at the first experiment on our liberties. Who does not see that the same authority which can establish Christianity, in exclusion of all other religions, may establish with the same ease any particular sect of Christians, in exclusion of all other sects? That the same authority which can force a citizen to contribute three pence only of his property for the support of any one establishment, may force him to conform to any other establishment in all cases whatsoever?"

The position of "neutrality" advocated by some is not the solution to the existing controversies. Our Constitution is not neutral in matters concerning basic values since freedom of religion and of conscience is an explicit postulate demanding active interaction and not passive neutrality. Neutrality can be applied only toward differences in the interpretation of ideas and practices by churches of various denominations as to what is permitted by the Scriptures and toward differences in catechisms, creeds, symbols, and confessional standards developed by the practices and beliefs of various churches. These differences cannot be settled by the coercive rule of secular law and must be left to the free conscience of each individual.

The presidential election of 1960 brought into clearer focus than any event before or since the issue of loyalty to the church and of loyalty to the state in

American political life. In the history of this country, John F. Kennedy was only the second Roman Catholic to be nominated for the presidency. At the time of his nomination, there was a heated controversy about the capability of a Catholic President to preserve his independence from the hierarchy in performing his duties.

The most notable instance of Kennedy's desire to address this issue was the famous meeting with the Greater Houston Ministerial Association on September 12, 1960. Kennedy made an opening statement and accepted questions from the floor from the Protestant ministers gathered. His stand on the issue was forthright:

"I believe in an America where the separation of church and state is absolute—where no Catholic prelate would tell the President (should he be a Catholic) how to act and no Protestant minister would tell his parishioners for whom to vote— where no church or church school is granted any public funds or political preference—and where no man is denied public office merely because his religion differs from the President who might appoint him or the people who might elect him.

"I believe in an America that is officially neither Catholic, Protestant, nor Jewish—where no public official either requests or accepts instructions on public policy from the Pope, the National Council of Churches or any other ecclesiastical source— where no religious body seeks to impose its will directly or indirectly upon the general populace or the public acts of its officials—and where religious liberty is so indivisible that an act against one church is treated as an act against all." (Theodore H. White, *The Making of the President 1960*, Atheneum Publishers, 1961, Appendix C, p. 391.)

Kennedy apparently convinced enough voters of his independence from clerical dictate that he received from Protestants more than half of the votes that elected him. (*Ibid.*, p. 357.)

Churches have always been involved in public policy and have always addressed the moral aspects of political issues. The abolitionist movement, prohibition, women's suffrage, the conservation of natural resources, the control of monopolies, and public education are all causes which have concerned many groups of mainline Protestants since the birth of our nation. In the early 1960s, the social activism of the churches played a major role in the passage of national civil rights legislation. In recent times the broadening agendas of churches' involvement include positions on abortion, homosexuality, pornography, the feminist movement, teaching of evolution and creationism, and even preoccupation with foreign affairs. Religious forces and values derived from religion have been the essential foundation for our form of government and among the important formative influences on our conduct.

The voice of the churches on issues with major moral content has penetrated various areas of public and private life. As believers in free enterprise, we have come to the realization that the completely uncontrolled process of a "free" economy may cause massive human sufferings when the idea of "free" enterprise becomes an absolute dogma. Compassion for the poor thus became a mark of our nation's tradition, and poverty became ethically intolerable. Unemployment insurance, Social Security, antipoverty measures, Medicare, and housing bills evidence the acceptance of the government's—as well as society's—responsibility for the poor and for the sick, a responsibility based on moral values nurtured by the churches.

On the international stage, an increased spiritual involvement on the part of church leaders in political life is evident. Catholic bishops of the Philippines condemned the fraud in the 1986 election and called on the Filipino people to vote their consciences despite intimidation and bribes and to rectify elections described as "unparalleled in the fraudulence of their conduct." After the February 7 elections, the pastoral letter of the Catholic bishops of the Philippines of February 14, 1986, declared that "a government that assumes or retains power through fraudulent means has no moral basis."

Cardinal Jaime Sin, the so-called father of the Philippine revolution, urged the people to show "solidarity" and "support" for the opposition in its attempt to unseat President Ferdinand Marcos. He took an active role in the events leading up to Marcos' fleeing the country. Sin urged Filipinos to form a protective wall around military leaders who had defected from Marcos' army.

Some Catholic circles in the Philippines dissented from the bishops' statement that declared the illegitimacy of the government and called for its overthrow, objecting to this statement as a dangerous step which invaded the political realm and violated the principle of the separation of church and state. The churchmen who joined Cardinal Sin in endorsing the bishops' pastoral letter of February 14 took the position that the church cannot be impartial in matters of morality and honesty, and silence would mean sanctioning the evils of cheating and harassment witnessed during the election. Politics is a human activity, and when people are in danger of being harmed, they maintained, the church has the obligation to speak on behalf of the sanctity of the ballot and to see that human rights are protected.

Moral judgments on a government made by the church are becoming ever more widespread. In Poland we witnessed a moral alliance of the opposition movement known as Solidarity and of the Catholic Church. Solidarity was born in 1979 as a consequence of Pope John Paul II's visit to Poland, described as "Poland's second baptism." It restored the dignity of the people oppressed by the communist regime, and the changed spirit of the Poles gave birth to a movement defending the rights of the worker and upholding fundamental social and moral principles.

Solidarity's policies of openness and nonviolence gained strong support from the Catholic Church. Although it was not one of Solidarity's goals to overthrow the government, Moscow could not tolerate the existence of such a movement enjoying overwhelming national support and the wide participation of the working class. Since Solidarity's dedication to liberty could have ignited the sparks of independence, it was banned by the Polish communist government. The "state of war" declared by the

government against Solidarity was followed by mass
arrests and imprisonment. The victims of this "war"
were Solidarity's leaders—among them Catholic
priests who participated in the movement opposed to
the totalitarian rule of the Polish version of the Soviet
regime.

In Nicaragua, Cardinal Miguel Olando y Bravo
strongly opposed the Somoza dictatorship and
denounced its crimes and abuses. He played a significant spiritual role in the Sandinista revolution but did
not hesitate to denounce the communist government
of Nicaragua that grasped power after the revolution
for the destruction of the goals of the revolution and of
the foundations on which democracy rests. He
rejected the legitimacy of the communist government
and accused it of mixing and confusing the concepts of
faith, the church, the revolution, *Sandinisma*, and the
fatherland. The Cardinal's position was challenged
and subverted by a group of priests who joined the
communist government. Some even became members of the cabinet in defiance of the Pope and the
Vatican hierarchy.

This fusion of religion and active participation in
politics, especially the holding of elective offices by
priests, has been condemned by the Vatican, which
saw in such office holding both a conflict in what
priests should represent to the faithful and a weakening of this mission caused by their belonging to one
party over another. The so-called liberation theology—which asserts that the church should engage in a
political struggle for social change—was rejected by
Pope John Paul II and other Vatican leaders who

believe that the priests should not be involved in direct political action in order to help the poor.

In his concern with the grave questions of social justice and equity in personal, national, and international relations, John Paul II expects the church to play a specific and important role which cannot be identified with nor replaced by the aim of politicians, sociologists, or business or union leaders. The priests who go beyond their role in speaking out on human justice, poverty, hunger, and alienation and take direct political action are not following the directions of Rome.

In Latin America, where nearly half of the world's Catholics live in widespread poverty and most contend with frequent guerrilla wars, the Vatican's views seem irrelevant to priests who are found on the front line of violent social struggle. The vast Latin American movement which is subsumed under the epithet "liberation theology" has therefore arisen and has been condemned by the Vatican for its deformation of theological principles and its disloyalty to the church and to the Pope, who in 1870 was declared by the First Vatican Council to be "endowed with that infallibility which according to the will of the Redeemer, is vouchsafed to the Church when she desires to fix a doctrine of faith or morality." On the televised visit of Pope John Paul II in Nicaragua, the Minister of Culture, Father Ernesto Cardinal, appeared on the screen kneeling before the Pope for a blessing. The Pope, wagging a finger of reproach, sternly reminded him that he must straighten out (*arreglar*) his relations with the Vatican.

In the United States, because of the opposition of the Vatican to having priests in elective office, Rev. Robert Drinan, a Massachusetts congressman—in order to comply with the order issued by Vatican officials to all priests throughout the world to cease secular political activism—in 1980 decided to withdraw from his congressional race to the great disappointment of his friends, aides, and some of the voters in Brookline, Massachusetts. For the same reasons, the Rev. Robert J. Cornell, who was attempting to regain the U.S. House seat from Wisconsin's Eighth District, gave up his candidacy for Congress as a result of Pope John Paul II's desire to enforce church law that discourages partisan political activity by clergy.

The holding of elective office by clergymen is not a new issue. Alexis de Tocqueville in his *Democracy in America,* the greatest book ever written by a foreigner about America, was surprised to discover that priests and ministers held no public appointments in this country in the early nineteenth century. There was not a single one in the administration, and they were not even represented in the assemblies. As to the attitudes of the clergy, he found that "most of them seemed voluntarily to steer clear of power and to take a sort of professional pride in claiming that it was no concern of theirs." (Tocqueville, p. 272.)

Tocqueville pointed out that this resistance to governmental service by clergymen was not solely voluntary or customary. The constitutions of such states as New York, Virginia, North and South Carolina, Kentucky, Tennessee, and Louisiana specifically prohibited the holding of office by clergymen during the time in which Tocqueville wrote. Article VII, Section 4, of the Constitution of New York of 1821 provided:

"And whereas the ministers of the gospel are, by their profession, dedicated to the service of God and the cure of souls and ought not to be diverted from the great duties of their functions, therefore, no minister of the gospel or priest of any denomination whatever . . . be eligible to or capable of holding any civil or military office or place within this state."

Tocqueville's observations about mingling religion with politics are pertinent to our times. Man, he wrote, shows a natural disgust for existence and an immense longing to exist; he fears annihilation and at the same time scorns life. "These different instincts constantly drive his soul toward contemplation of the next world, and it is religion that leads him thither. Religion, therefore, is only one particular form of hope, and it is as natural to the human heart as hope itself . . . ; faith is the permanent state of mankind."

Having described religion as one of the constituent principles of human nature, Tocqueville reaches the following conclusion:

"When a religion seeks to found its sway only on the longing for immortality equally tormenting every human heart, it can aspire to universality; but when it comes to uniting itself with a government, it must adopt maxims which apply only to certain nations. Therefore, by allying itself with

any political power, religion increases its strength
over some but forfeits the hope of reigning over
all.

"As long as a religion relies only upon the
sentiments which are the consolation of every
affliction, it can draw the heart of mankind to
itself. When it is mingled with the bitter passions
of this world, it is sometimes constrained to
defend allies who are such from interest rather
than from love; and it has to repulse as adversaries
men who still love religion, although they are
fighting against religion's allies. Hence religion
cannot share the material strength of the rulers
without being burdened with some of the animos-
ity roused against them." (*Ibid.*, p. 273.)

Tocqueville's conclusions recall those that Edmund
Burke expressed in 1790 in his famous *Reflections on
the French Revolution*. Burke's essay grew out of his
response to a sermon preached by a Unitarian
minister, Dr. Richard Price, who had praised the
Revolution from the pulpit. Burke's remarks are a
classic summation of the dangers of fusing religion
with politics and of the problem of loyalty to the
church versus loyalty to a political cause:

". . . [P]olitics and the pulpit are terms that have
little agreement. No sound ought to be heard in
the church but the healing voice of Christian
charity. The cause of civil liberty and civil government gains as little as that of religion by this confu-
sion of duties. Those who quit their proper
character, to assume what does not belong to
them, are for the greater part, ignorant both of the

character they leave, and of the character they assume. Wholly unacquainted with the world in which they are so fond of meddling, and inexperienced in all its affairs, on which they pronounce with so much passion, they have nothing of politics but the passions they excite. Surely the church is a place where one day's truce ought to be allowed to the dissensions and animosities of mankind." (*Reflections on the French Revolution,* P. F. Collier & Son, 1909, p. 160.)

Since free institutions derive much of their moral vitality from religion, it is the responsibility of the church to enter the public arena to nurture the broad moral values on which the foundation of our democracy rests. The chief mission of the church is to develop the individual's religious conscience; an attempt to advise him on the adequacy of machinery to be used in domestic or international relations will only hinder the role of the church. It is not the responsibility of the church to endorse legislation or policies which involve technical elements that call for special knowledge and experience.

It is outside the intellectual and moral competence of the clergy to advise parishioners whether they should buy gold krugerrands or push United States investments in South Africa, as a Protestant minister suggested upon his return from that country. It is outside the objective of ethical concern to recommend changes in lending policies of the World Bank and the International Monetary Fund, as did the 1986 pastoral letter of the National Conference of Catholic Bishops called "Economic Justice for All." The church may promote free education in order to provide all youth with the right to equal opportunities to develop their capabilities. No one expects, however, that the church is well equipped to suggest what kind of state or federal offices should be engaged in extending aid to education.

Old age and ill health have always been of genuine concern to the church, but is it the responsibility of the church to act as an arbiter on the organization of Medicare or of Social Security, which involves technical elements that call for special knowledge and experience? Freedom of association calls for the right to organize labor unions, but the authority of the church is undermined when it calls either for support or for repeal of the "right to work" laws. This caution should also apply to international relations, where it is necessary to deal with existing realities and practical measures which do not always fulfill the church's visions of and aspirations for justice.

The relationship of the City of God to the City of Man can be compared with the use of a compass in navigation. A compass points the way to a destination but is not expected to solve practical problems of navigation. Similarly, the church is admirably fitted to pointing toward the ends society should strive for but should not be expected to identify the technical means, an act demanding training and experience, by which those ends should be reached. The noble ends of spiritual life are often difficult to harmonize with the reality of domestic problems and international relations. At home we accept only with a certain suspicion—whether justified or not—the assurances of moral motives and spiritual purpose from those who are professionally active in political life. On the international stage, if the City of Man unreservedly adopts the lofty principles embodied in the Sermon on the Mount, it may find itself defenseless against the evils posed by the forces of totalitarianism with its military machines aimed at the destruction of the Free World.

There is always the peril of brutalizing the City of God by associating it with the game of politics in the City of Man. The City of God loses its spiritual purity when it associates itself with man-made dogmas and the means used in the City of Man to succeed in practical politics. Had the Church allowed itself to become the champion of changing political or economic theories, it would have suffered the fate of these passing dogmas. Calvin's idea of social reconstruction through the iron supervision of the omnipotent church—which would include control of markets, crafts, rents, interest, prices, and all other economic activities—was later decried as tyranny of the clergy. In Iran the emergence of a theocratic social order is marked with a brutality characteristic only of totalitarian regimes that reject religion as an operative part of social ideas. The two cities should be kept apart.

Loyalty and Academic Freedom

The widespread student unrest which we witnessed in the late 1960s and early 1970s—which was encouraged in many quarters by members of institutional faculties—spawned renewed discussion about the compatibility of loyalty to our nation with academic freedom. Can these two values, each essential to democracy, be preserved without sacrificing loyalty in the interest of academic freedom or without imposing any straitjacket on the intellectual leaders in our colleges and universities in the interest of loyalty? This question is not characteristic only of the times of the campus disorders; it was also discussed in the early days of our nation. When on March 4, 1825, the first classes met at the new University of Virginia, Jefferson's resolution on the "principles which are to be taught" was condemned by some of his critics as an imposition of a partisan yoke of loyalty on the educational life of the University.

Jefferson, the rector of the new school, offered in his resolution a list of six books or documents underlying, in the opinion of the Board of Visitors, principles of government which should be "inculcated" and that are "generally approved by our fellow citizens." John Locke's *Essay concerning the true original extent and end of civil government* and Algernon Sidney's *Discourses on Government* were recommended for their treatment of "the general principles of liberty and the rights of man in nature and in society." The "best guides" to the "distinctive principles of the government" were to be found in the remaining four: (1) the Declaration of Independence, as "the fundamental act of union" of the United States; (2) the book known by the title of *The Federalist*, "being an authority to which appeal is habitually made by all, and rarely declined or denied by any as evidence of the general opinion of those who framed, and of those who accepted the Constitution of the U.S. on questions as to its genuine meaning"; (3) the Resolution of the General Assembly of Virginia in 1799, on the subject of the Alien and Sedition Laws, "which appeared in accord with the predominant sense of the people of the U.S."; and (4) the valedictory address of President Washington, "as conveying political lessons of peculiar value."

The preamble of the resolution declared that it is the duty of the University's board to provide that none of the principles of government "be inculcated which are incompatible with those on which the Constitution of this state and of the U.S. were genuinely based, in the common opinion." For this reason the board found it necessary to point out the sources where the principles of government "are to be found legitimately developed." The books and documents suggested by the resolution, except for the Virginia Resolutions of 1798 – 1799 drafted by Jefferson and Madison, hardly present partisan political philosophies. Alexander Hamilton, who bitterly opposed Jefferson and was openly antagonistic to his interpretation of the Constitution, was one of the main contributors to *The Federalist*. However, the preamble's provision that forbade teaching principles that are unreconcilable with those on which the Constitution's are based, "in the common opinion," was capable of encroaching upon the freedom of communication of ideas, particularly in the academic environment.

The concept of "common opinion" tends to impinge upon the sensitive area of freedom of inquiry.

As the U.S. Supreme Court pointed out, "No field of education is so thoroughly comprehended by man that new discoveries cannot yet be made. Particularly is that true in the social sciences, where few, if any, principles are accepted as absolutes. . . . Teachers and students must always remain free to inquire, to study and to evaluate, to gain new maturity and understanding; otherwise our civilization will stagnate and die." (*Sweezy v. State of New Hampshire*, 354 U.S. 234, 250, 77 S. Ct. 1203, 1211 – 1212 [1957].)

Academic freedom is indispensable to a democratic society. It gives vitality to the process of learning and teaching. Unorthodoxy or dissent may be in the vanguard of democratic thought, and the absence of such voices may be a symptom of grave apathy in our society. Does this mean that academic freedom permits disregard for certain established moral standards in the processes of inquiry and thought? Not at all. It is subject to conditions which maintain the essential purpose of a university, which is to seek the truth.

A qualified person who seeks to fulfill the mission of a university by searching for truth has the right to teach conclusions that seem to him reasonably valid in the light of objective scholarship and intellectual integrity. This academic freedom carries with it duties correlative with rights. The 1940 Basic Statement on Academic Freedom of the American Association of University Professors states, "The teacher is entitled to freedom in the classroom in discussing his subject but should be careful not to introduce into his teaching controversial matter which has no relation to his subject." In 1956, the AAUP asserted, "The academic community has a duty to defend society and itself from subversion of the educational process by dishonest tactics, including political conspiracies to deceive students and lead them into acceptance of dogmas or false causes."

Academic freedom is not a citizen's birthright. It is a right that must be earned and can be enjoyed only by those who meet standards of qualification that are an indispensable condition of professional performance. Academic freedom is granted only to scholars truly seeking to reach the truth by applying objective scholarship, not to propagandists who try to dictate their political views and use the classrooms for political purposes. As long as academic freedom is not used to subvert the educational process "by dishonest tactics, including political conspiracies" leading to the acceptance of poisonous and false dogmas, there is no conflict between academic freedom and loyalty to the nation.

In a democractic society there will always be controversial issues, but the focus of both loyalty and academic freedom is the same; search for the truth and progress of society through the progress of knowledge. The focus of both is the pursuit of truth and originality and the acceptance of duties and responsibilities as a correlative to the right of academic freedom and to the rights of citizenship. Loyalty and academic freedom call for commitment to preserving our cultural values and to nurturing the means for responsible reform of social institutions based upon established standards of moral judgment.

Loyalty—An Essential Virtue in a Democracy

In my book *Three Sources of National Strength,* patriotism was identified as one of those sources. Loyalty to the nation was listed as one of the virtues distinctive to patriotism, since it means the fidelity that emanates from a love of and devotion to one's country. The most important aspects involved in loyalty to the nation and to the government discussed in that book are pertinent to my arguments concerning the role of loyalty in the cultivation of democracy and in the life of the individual.

Loyalty to the nation must be single-hearted and not compromised by a loyalty to any other country. A person desiring citizenship in the United States, for instance, must renounce his allegiance to another nation and to any foreign sovereign. Such single-heartedness, however, does not prevent an interest in international order and in the well-being of other nations. Just as familial love and devotion do not preclude concern for those outside the family, loyalty to one's nation is compatible with an interest in alleviating the suffering of those in other parts of the world and in building a world of stability and progress.

History reminds us of many occasions on which American patriots made sacrifices both of their treasure and of their very lives in order to assist others throughout the world. One of the recent examples of this willingness to sacrifice for the freedom of others occurred in the years after World War II, when the United States not only sent relief aid to those whose lives had been ravaged by the war but also enabled the nations of both Europe and Asia—including defeated enemies—to rebuild their economies and to restore democracy and freedom where once tyranny had reigned. The meaning of patriotic loyalty translated into powerful forces for good in the world was expressed by George Santayana: "A man's feet must be planted in this country, but his eyes should survey the world."

Loyalty to the nation does not always mean loyalty to any given government. Patriotic loyalty may take the form of a conscientious stand against a regime that uses its coercive power to enforce its authority to oppress its own people. In this century, we have seen many heroic men and women who refused to surrender their consciences to tyrants and defied pernicious totalitarian governments. They answered the call to a higher loyalty to their nations when they sacrificed their lives rather than declare their allegiance to totalitarian rulers. (For a more detailed discussion of loyalty to the nation and to the government, see Cecil, *Three Sources of National Strength*, The University of Texas at Dallas, 1986, pp. 110–121.)

The fact that loyalty is a centralizing motive in an individual's personal life does not mean that it affects the development of the individual's conscience or of his moral will or that it excuses him from individual responsibility. An appeal to loyalty succeeds as a tool of oppression by tyrants only when an individual gives up his right to independent judgment. When a country is brutalized by a tyrant who demands loyalty from his oppressed subjects, the individual seeking freedom is guided by the vision of those who aspire to